Social Media for Professionals

Establish Your Professional

Identity Online

By Rob Ganjon

Social Media for Professionals – Establish Your Professional Identity Online

© Copyright 2011, Rob Ganjon

Table of Contents

Introduction

In March 2011 I was sitting in a meeting at American Express with a couple dozen executives talking about social media. We had brought in a few young managers to talk about how they use social media. As I watched these successful and smart executives ask questions, it was clear that several of them were not using the most popular social media platforms like Twitter, LinkedIn, etc. They wanted to be on these platforms, but they just didn't know how to get started.

As I thought about it, I wondered how many other executives out there were feeling the same way. That's when I decided to create a how-to guide aimed at getting professionals and executives online with a drop-dead simple guide. And that's what this is. By the end of this book, you should be fully on-line with complete profiles on the four most relevant social platforms for working professionals – Facebook, Twitter, LinkedIn and Tumblr.

Why is this important? Business usage of social media and online networking is exploding, with professionals and organizations of all shapes and sizes worldwide joining the social media revolution.

This guide to social media will help you start incorporating social media and online networking to further your career, by establishing your online identity as an integrated part of your overall career strategy.

Why should you use social media? One key benefit is simply to be found more often by potential clients or employers, who today expect that you will have an online presence. Online networking and social media offer you a fantastic opportunity and a new way of connecting with colleagues and potential employers in a two-way dialogue.

For many professionals, social media is a cost-effective alternative to physical networking. Social media also boosts your search results, again helping your professional expertise to be found online. For example, Google tracks Twitter and blogs in its search results, making your professional credentials more prominent when people Google your name. What will employers find when they Google your name?

Recruiters and HR managers were among the first to embrace social media and to use these channels to search out professional candidates on the business networking site LinkedIn.com and to cross-check their credibility and background on online platforms such as Facebook and Twitter. For executives and job-hunters, it is now important to establish your "personal brand" online to build your career.

Let's look quickly at the facts and statistics on social media in 2011. The clear leader is Facebook, with over 750 million members worldwide, and I'm sure that number is even higher by the time you read this. If Facebook was a country, it would be the world's 3rd largest. Twitter gained 30 million new members just in the last 3 months of 2010 alone, and it continues to grow steadily.

Social media now accounts for 1 in each 4 ½ minutes spent online, and the fastest-growing demographics are in the 30+ and 50+ age groups—your potential customers and colleagues. Your future clients may also include people under 30 who wouldn't know what to do with a phone book, but who automatically go online to find the companies and information they are looking for.

There are many ways that you can use social media to establish and promote your professional credibility, including just as a starting point:

- Creating online business profiles

- Posting updates, links, alerts, photos, videos, and special offers
- Building your professional and local networks
- Reaching new potential customers
- Relationship-building with existing customers and contacts
- Building new email marketing databases
- Blogging and/or tweeting in your expert area
- Monitoring positive/negative feedback and responding
- Answering customer/public questions
- Setting up an additional customer service channel

Online and social networking should now be an integral part of a strategy for most professionals and businesses. By taking a look at four of the most popular social media and online networking outlets—Facebook, Twitter, LinkedIn, and Tumblr—this book will take you step by step through the process of setting up an account for each of these sites to optimally enhance the professional credibility.

How to Use This Book (make sure you read this!)

This book was written to help professionals create their profiles on the major social media sites – Facebook, LinkedIn, Twitter and Tumblr. It's designed for people who want a little extra help getting started or a little more assistance navigating these sites and completing their profiles. To that end, what you'll find in this book is some extra guidance to complement each site's setup wizard. Helpful tips and additional instruction aimed at guiding a user through each site's enrollment and set up process.

This is not a book you should read cover to cover and it's certainly not something you should take to the beach with you (at least I wouldn't). While you'll find some basic information about the sites and about social media in general, don't expect to find a lot of wizbang social media strategy in this book. This book won't give you the top 10 ways to market your business on Twitter or the secrets to using LinkedIn to land your dream job in 30 days.

Instead, you should think of this book as an instruction manual. When you're ready to set up your Tumblr account, have this book with you at your computer. Open it up to the Tumblr section and use the book to guide you through the account set up process. If you're the type of person that finds yourself saying things like "what does it want me to do now?" or "this site doesn't make any sense", this book should help you out. If it doesn't, let me know.

Good Luck!

FACEBOOK

Facebook – An Introduction

Attracting 41% of all social media traffic in 2011, Facebook is the world's largest online social community, with over 750 million members worldwide and continuing to grow strongly. An average Facebook user is on the site approximately six hours a week.

Individuals set up personal profiles on Facebook to connect with friends, family, contacts, and others through features, including status updates, wall posts, uploading photos and videos, joining groups like yours, reading news feeds, and sending messages.

Additionally, users can search for people whom they are interested in communicating with. They can add other users as friends, exchange messages, and receive notifications when they update their profiles. They can view comments, photographs, and post comments on their friend's updates. This all comes with the level of security the user wants.

Some of the key features of Facebook are the following:

❖ **Wall**
Wall is a space on your profile page that allows friends to post messages for you, and it displays the time and date the message was written.

❖ **Photos & Videos**
You can upload photos and videos, and you can also upload albums of photos, tag friends helped by face recognition technology, and comment on photos.

❖ **Status Updates**
You can post messages for all your friends to read. In turn, friends can respond with their own comments, and they can also press the "Like" button to show that they enjoyed reading it.

❖ **Networks, Groups, and "Like Pages"**
There are different networks and groups you can join. Privacy settings are possible on the basis of networks. You can create "Like Pages," which allows fans of an individual, organization, product, service, or concept to join a Facebook fan club.

❖ **News Feed**
News feed highlights any change in information, like profile changes, upcoming events, and birthdays—among other updates.

❖ **Notification**
If someone is sharing a link on your wall or commenting on a post you previously commented on, you get notified.

❖ **Deals**
You can see online deals and/or available coupons from various business houses, or you can take part in business campaigns.

❖ **Messages and Inbox**
You can send and receive messages using the messages feature.

Ways You Can Use Facebook

If you own a business, you can build their presence on the site by setting up a "Facebook Page," as business profiles are known. This becomes your Facebook hub, connecting you with individuals, businesses and potential customers, who join your Page to share, discuss, and support—also boosting traffic to your own website.

Some ways your business can use Facebook are the following:

• Building new customer and marketing databases
• Promoting special offers, new product alerts
• Visually highlighting your work—upload videos and pictures
• Listening and responding to customers

7

- Events—announce, promote, handle RSVPs, etc.
- Local/location-based marketing
- Targeted advertising

Best Practices and Tips for Using Facebook

Integrate your Facebook activity with your other online activity. Facebook is generally thought of as a personal and social website, and less of a professional networking site. People tend to use Facebook more for connecting with friends and family and less for connecting with colleagues and employers. But these lines are blurring more and more every day. The important thing to remember is that potential employers, colleagues and customers may be just a click away from your Facebook page, so keep that in mind when you're using the site.

Some starting points to help you make the most of your Facebook presence include the following:

- Design your Facebook page and profile in a way that defines your personal brand. Be true to who you are and what you stand for, but avoid putting too much emphasis on areas that you wouldn't want to be front and center with potential employers.

- Be active—regularly post updates, photos, videos and exclusive content to stimulate comments and "likes."

- Build relationships—check your page quickly each day to listen, learn from your community, and respond to comments.

- Join and participate on other Pages where audiences overlap. Being seen as connected, friendly, and an expert others can approach in your specialist area is important.

How to Set Up a Facebook Account

This section is a step-by-step guide for opening a Facebook account, completing a Facebook profile, and getting started with managing friends.

> ➤ **Registration**

To create a user profile on Facebook, you have to open an account with Facebook, which is absolutely free. The Facebook registration process is described below.

Open a new browser window. You can use any browser like Internet Explorer, Chrome, Firefox, etc. I am using Internet Explorer here. Enter the URL www.Facebook.com in the browser address bar and press **Enter**.

The Facebook Home Page is displayed as shown below:

> **Sign Up**

To start the registration process, fill in the information under "Sign Up." In order to be eligible to sign up for Facebook, users must be thirteen (13) years of age or older.

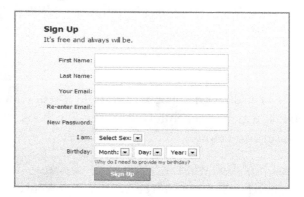

Complete the entries in the fields. The following table provides more information:

This Field	Requires...
First Name	Enter your first name. First name and the last name will be displayed in your profile as your username. Your connections will see your first and last name.
Last Name	Enter your last name.
Your Email	Enter your email address. This will be your primary email address. This is the address you will log in with. Facebook will deliver all email messages regarding invitations, requests, and other system mails to this email address. You can have one Facebook account per email address.
Re-enter Email	Enter your email address again. This is to confirm that the email address is correct.
New Password	Enter your password.
I am	Select your sex: "Male" or "Female."
Birthday	Select your birthday month, day, and year.
Sign Up	Click the **Sign Up** button.

The Security Check page will then be displayed.

➢ **Security Check**

The Security Check page prompts you to write the letters displayed in the text box. You also have an option of listening to an audio impulse and the writing the text as per what you hear.

Complete the entry in the field. The following table provides more information:

This Field	Requires...
Try different words	Clicking on this link changes the words written in the text box. You can do this when the words in the box are not clearly visible. You can re-enter the new set of words in the text box.
audio captcha	Clicking on this link lets you hear the text words to be entered. Enter the words you hear in the text box.
Text in the box	Enter the text shown in the box above or the ones you hear from 'audio captcha.'

This Field	Requires...
Sign Up	Click **Sign Up** to get started.

Once you click **Sign Up**, you get started and are taken to the "Find Friends" page. An email with the subject "Just one more step to get started on Facebook" gets sent to your account immediately to complete your sign-up process.

Note: You can continue to fill in your profile information without clicking on the link sent in the email. It is just an intermediate email that has links to help you go directly to the fields that are important to create an account. In case you don't click this email and continue to fill in profile information, another email will be sent with the subject "'Welcome to Facebook."

➢ **Find Friends**

This page prompts you to search contacts among your existing Yahoo!, rediff, or other email accounts. This is completely optional and can be skipped if you feel uncomfortable giving your password. Once you enter your other email address and password, you will be able to import your contacts to Facebook.

The following table provides information about the fields:

This Field	Requires...
Your Email	Your email address as entered in the "Sign Up" screen will automatically show up in this text box.
Find Friends	This button and link takes you to the login page of the respective email service website. You can fill in your password and import your contact list.
Other Email Service	After clicking the **Other Email Service** option, a pop-up window appears prompting you to enter your other email address and password. The contacts are similarly imported from that website. After clicking the **Find Friends** button, the contacts get imported into Facebook contacts.

Facebook searches for the contacts in your email account and displays the contacts that are on Facebook. You can add them as Friends, as shown in the figure below:

Select the friends you want to add by clicking on the respective check boxes and click the **Add Friends** button.

The "Invite Friends and Family to Facebook" page is displayed. You can invite other contacts to Facebook as shown in the figure below.

Select the check boxes of the contacts you want to invite to Facebook and click the **Send Invites** button. Facebook will send invites to these contacts via email.

The "Find Friends" page is displayed again as shown in the figure on the next page.

You can continue to search contacts in another email account or you can click **Skip this step** to proceed to the next step: "Profile Information."

➢ **Profile Information**

The profile information allows you to fill information about your high school, college/university, and employers (previous and current). This information helps others on Facebook to find you. Filling out this information is not compulsory.

The following table provides more information on fields to be filled:

This Field	Requires...
High School	Enter the name of the high school you went to and further details.
College/University	Enter the name of the college or university that you went to and further details.
Employers	Enter your employers name and details.
Save and Continue	Entries get stored as part of your profile.
Skip	Go to the next section as none of this is mandatory.
Back	You will go back to the previous page.

➤ **High School**

As you start typing, Facebook suggests groups/networks of schools already registered. If you find the school you are looking for, you can select it. If you do not find your entry in the list, you can simply click on **Add <<name of your school>>** as shown in the figure below. You can add more than one school.

As soon as you select the school from the list, you see further detailing. A few text boxes appear, allowing you to enter further details like the year and with whom you have studied.

The following table provides more information on fields to be filled:

This Field	Requires...
Class Year	Select the year in which you studied at the school.
With	Enter the name of other persons with whom you studied.
Add School	After pressing the **Add School** button, the data gets saved as part of your profile under the "Education and Work" section.
Cancel	Press the **Cancel** button to clear the school details.

If you do not find your entry in the list, you can simply click on **Add <<name of your school>>**.

➤ **College/University**

As you start typing, Facebook suggests groups/networks of colleges/universities already registered. If you find the one you are looking for, you can select it. If you do not find your entry in the list, you can write the name of your college/university and add it.

You can select more than one college or university. Filling College/University is not mandatory.

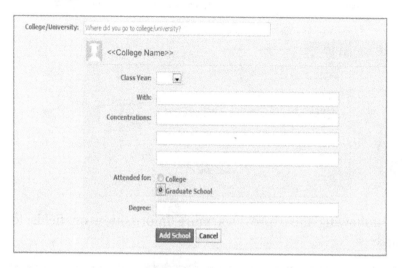

The following table provides more information on the fields to be filled:

This Field	Requires...
Class Year	Select the year in which you studied at the college/university.
With	Enter the name of other person(s) with whom you studied.
Concentrations	Enter the subjects you majored in or electives you took in college/ university.
Attended for	Select "College" or "Graduate School."
Degree	This appears only if you select "Graduate School" in the "Attended for" option. Enter your degree name.
Add School	After pressing the **Add School** button, the data gets saved as part of you profile under the "Education and Work" section.
Cancel	Press **Cancel** to clear all the entries made.

➢ Employer

Enter the name of your employer. As you start typing, Facebook suggests groups or networks that are already registered. If you find the one you are looking for, you can select it. If you do not find your entry in the list, you can write the name of your employer and add. You can add more than one Employer. Filling Employer information is not mandatory.

The following table provides more information on fields to be filled:

This Field	Requires...
Employer	Enter your employer's name.
Position	Enter your job designation or the position with the employer. Facebook gives suggestions below as you type on. Either you can select from them or continue to write your own.
City/Town	Enter your city or town name. Facebook gives suggestions below as you type on. Either you can select from them or continue to write your own.
With	Enter the name of other person(s) you worked with.
Description	Enter any additional data you want to write.

19

This Field	Requires...
I currently work here	You can either check or uncheck the square box.
Time Period	Select the month and year from the drop-down box.
Add Job	After pressing the **Add Job** button, the data gets saved as part of your profile under the "Education and Work" section.
Cancel	Press the **Cancel** button to clear all the entries made.

> **Profile Picture**

The Profile Picture page allows you to upload your photograph or the profile image that will be seen along with your username on Facebook. When you search Facebook for friends or contacts, the profile picture helps you to narrow down the person you are looking for. Uploading a profile picture is not mandatory to create an account. It is a feature provided by Facebook for the benefit of users. After successfully completing these steps, the user is taken to the "Welcome" screen of Facebook.

The "Set your profile picture" screen is displayed below:

You can browse your computer and upload an image as your profile picture. The picture can also be instantly clicked using the webcam on your computer.

> **Upload a Photo**

Click the **Upload a Photo** button, and the pop-up window "Upload Your Profile Picture" is displayed as shown in the figure below.

The following table provides more information on fields to be filled:

This Field	Requires...
Browse...	You can browse your computer and select an image. It gets saved as your profile picture.
Cancel	This option closes the current window and takes you back to the "Profile Picture" page.

> **Take a Profile Picture**

Your profile picture can instantly be taken using a webcam. Click the **Take a Profile Picture** button to get an instant image.

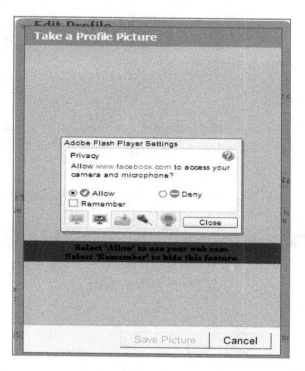

The following table provides more information on fields to be filled:

This Field	Requires...
Allow/Deny	This is the permission you need to give to the webcam. Select "Allow" for activating the webcam.
Remember	Check the "Remember" check box to ensure that the webcam doesn't ask for the permission again to activate the webcam.
Close	Press the **Close** button to close the window and the webcam starts.

The final page, as can be seen after uploading an image as an example a blank image), is uploaded here.

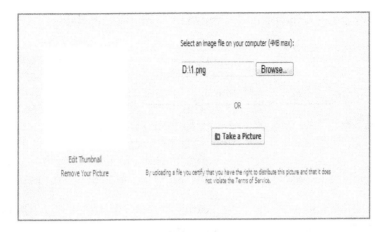

The following table provides more information on these fields:

This Field	Requires...
Edit Thumbnail	You can adjust your picture to fit best in thumbnail size.
Remove Your Picture	After clicking the **Remove Your Picture** option, the image is removed after confirmation.

➢ Edit Profile Picture

Once the photo is taken, you can edit it or remove it. As an example, a blank photo is taken below. The image can be edited. Click on the **Edit Thumbnail** option.

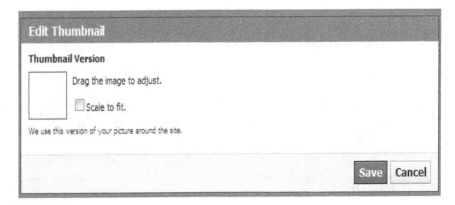

23

The following table provides more information on fields:

This Field	Requires...
Image	You can drag the image to adjust it as per the thumbnail size.
Scale to fit.	Checking this automatically fits your image to the thumbnail size.
Save	The edited image gets saved.
Cancel	It cancels the current operation and control goes back to the previous page.

You will be taken to the "Welcome" screen of Facebook. You have to log into your email account for confirmation. The page displays all the information you filled in the previous section. To change any of this information, you can click on their respective options.

The following table provides more information on fields:

This Field	Requires...
Go to your email	Click on this to go to your email account.
Find Friends	Press the **Find Friends** button to search for your friends from the email address contacts.

This Field	Requires...
Upload a profile picture	Shows the picture you uploaded and gives you the option to upload a new one or take a new picture.
Edit Profile	Takes you to the "Edit Profile" page.
Activate your mobile phone	The account registration gets confirmed after you give your mobile phone number. You can do this from a link provided in the email sent to you too.
Find people you know	Search your friends by entering their names.
Control what information you share	You can set account privacy settings and be selective in choosing what information you want to share with different groups of people.

> **Complete Sign-Up via Email**

An email with the subject "Just one more step to get started on Facebook" goes to the email address mentioned during sign-up. The link in the email assists you to finish the sign-up process.

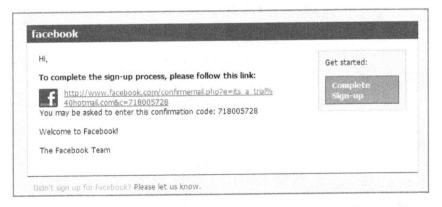

Clicking on the link in the email opens a new Facebook browser window, with you already logged in. You can activate your account by entering any of the following fields:

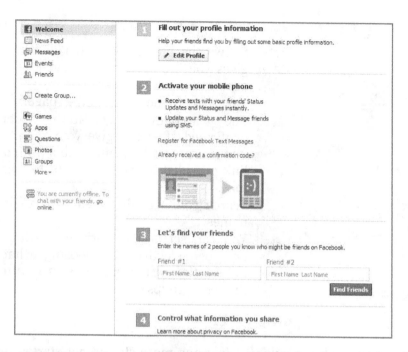

The following table provides information about the fields:

This Field	Requires...
Edit Profile	Clicking on this takes you to the "Edit Profile" page. Please refer to the "Edit Profile" section.
Activate your mobile phone: Register for Facebook Text Messages	This is needed to confirm your account on the mobile phone. You need to enter your phone number. A confirmation code is sent. You need to enter the confirmation code.
Activate your mobile phone: Already received a confirmation code?	After clicking, this window opens, prompting you to enter your confirmation code. It verifies and allows updates on your mobile phone.
Let's find your friends	Search your friends by entering their names.
Control what information you share	You can change your privacy settings to control the information you want to display.

Please go directly to the "Edit Profile" section for Profile Information and other options.

> ➢ **Activate Your Mobile Phone**

You can receive messages and updates on your phones if you register your phone number on Facebook.

The first step to activate your mobile phone is that you need to enter your country name and mobile carrier/service provider name.

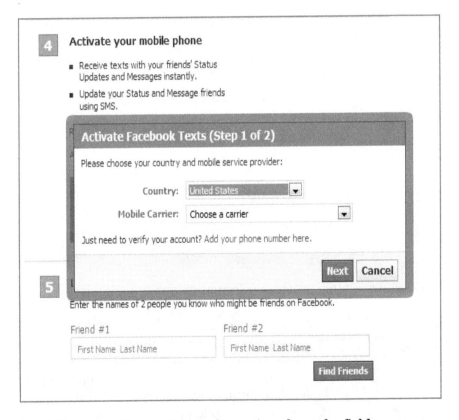

The following table provides information about the fields:

This Field	Requires...
Country	Select your country.

This Field	Requires...
Mobile Carrier	Select your mobile carrier.
Add your phone number here.	After clicking this link, a window opens with two fields: Country Code (a drop-down menu) and Phone Number (a text field). Enter your details and press the **Confirm** button.
Next	Go to the next step.

You can type F on your mobile and send it to 51555. A verification code is sent that you need to fill in the respective field.

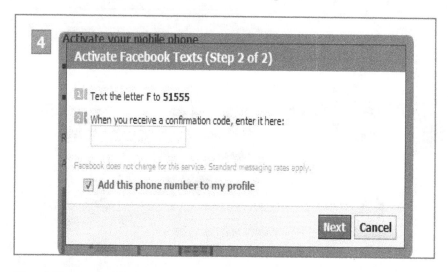

The following table provides information about the fields:

This Field	Requires...
Confirmation Code	Enter the confirmation code as received from Facebook.
Add this phone number to my profile	You can add the mobile number for future messages and notifications.
Next	The code gets verified and activates your mobile phone for Facebook.

➤ Edit Profile

You can click on the **Edit Profile** option on your Facebook home page to fill in additional information about yourself. This helps the application in suggesting the various network and people whom you would like to be in contact with.

The details you had filled in previously will get automatically populated in the respective fields, and they can be edited. Most of the text fields have suggestive existing entries to choose from.

Click the "Profile" tab on the Facebook Home page, as shown in the figure below.

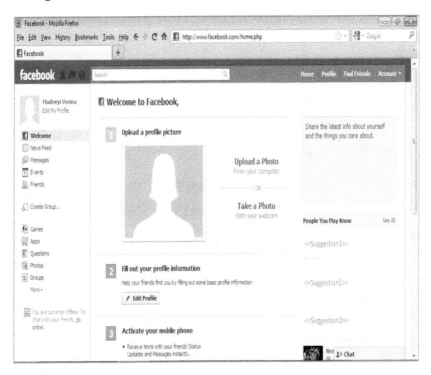

Your Profile page is displayed as shown in the figure below.

29

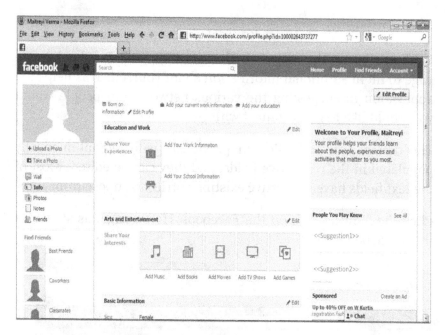

Click the **Edit Profile** button to add more information to your profile that will help your friends and family find you.

➢ **Basic Information**

The Basic Information screen is displayed below.

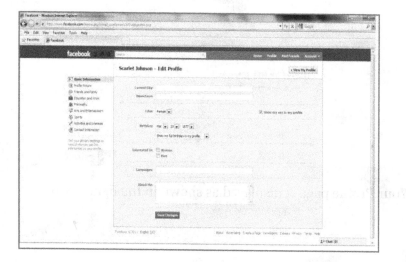

The following table provides more information on fields:

This Field	Requires...
Current City	Enter your current city. Facebook gives you choices as you type in the entry. You can either select your choice or type your text.
Hometown	Enter your hometown. Facebook gives you choices as you type in the entry. You can either select your choice or type your text.
I am	Select "Male" or "Female."
Show my sex in my profile	Check or uncheck the square box to show or not show your sex respectively in your profile information page.
Birthday	Select the month, date and year of your birth from the drop-down menu. You can select "Show my full birthday profile," "Show only month and day in my profile," or "Don't show my birthday in my profile" from the drop-down box.
Interested In	Check or uncheck the box for "Men" or "Women."
Languages	Enter the languages you know. Facebook gives you choices as you type in the entry. You can either select your choice or type your text.
About Me	Enter any additional information you want.
Save Changes	Your entries get saved to your profile.

> **Profile Picture**

The Profile Picture screen is displayed below.

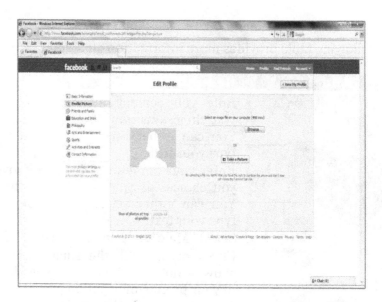

➤ Friends and Family

You can enter information about your friends and family and your particular relation with them. Facebook also sends friend request and invitations to the email addresses that you enter.

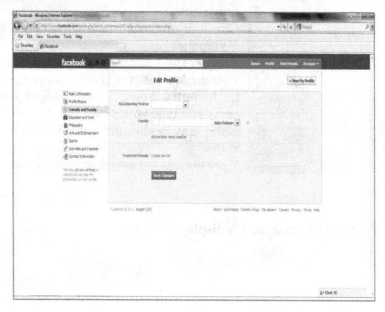

The following table provides more information on fields:

This Field	Requires...
Relationship Status	Select your relationship status from the drop-down menu.
Family	Enter the name of the family member in the text field.
Select Relation	Choose from the drop-down menu the relation that you have with the entry. Once you choose this, the Birthday (month, day, and year) drop-down populates. If you don't choose relation, a text box for friend's email address gets populated.
Featured Friends: Create new list	"Create new list" allows you to classify friends and family members under different list names.
Add an Existing List or Group	You can organize your friends on Facebook and create custom privacy settings. You can also use them to filter stories you see in News Feed.
Save Changes	Your changes get saved.

➢ **Education and Work**

The entries previously made will get populated. You can edit and save them in the same manner.

➢ Philosophy

This section allows you to enter your religion, political views, and any philosophical information or inclination that you would like to share.

The following table provides more information on the fields:

This Field	Requires...
Religion	Enter your religion. Facebook gives you choices as you type in the entry. You can either select your choice or type your text.
Description	Enter free text to describe your religion.
Political Views	Enter your political views. Facebook gives you choices as you type in the entry. You can either select your choice or type your text.
Description	Enter free text to describe your political views.
People Who Inspire You	Enter the name of people who inspire you. Facebook gives you choices as you type in the entry. You can either select your choice or type your text. You can select more than one entry.

This Field	Requires...
Favorite Quotations	Enter free text in the box.
Save Changes	Saves your entries.

> **Arts and Entertainment**

You can specify your interests in arts and entertainment. It allows you to choose and enter a variety of information like books, movies, etc.

The following table provides more information on fields:

This Field	Requires...
Music	Enter the type of music you like. Facebook gives you choices as you type in the entry. You can either select your choice or type your text. You can make multiple selections. They get listed in sequential order.
Books	Enter book names. Facebook gives you choices as you type in the entry. You can either select your choice or type your text. You can make multiple selections. They get listed in sequential order.

This Field	Requires...
Movies	Enter the name of the movies of your choice. Facebook gives you choices as you type in the entry. You can either select your choice or type your text. You can make multiple selections. They get listed in sequential order.
Television	Enter television programs. Facebook gives you choices as you type in the entry. You can either select your choice or type your text. You can make multiple selections. They get listed in sequential order.
Games	Enter your favorite games. Facebook gives you choices as you type in the entry. You can either select your choice or type your text. You can make multiple selections. They get listed in sequential order.
Save Changes	Saves your entries.

> **Sports**

You can add the sports you play. You can add details like your favorite team(s) and athletes. You can make multiple entries and drag them to change the sequence in which they appear.

The following table provides more information on fields:

This Field	Requires...
Sports You Play	Enter the name of sports that you play. Facebook gives you choices as you type in the entry. You can either select your choice or type your text. You can make multiple selections. They get listed in sequential order.
Favorite Teams	Enter the names of your favorite teams. Facebook gives you choices as you type in the entry. You can either select your choice or type your text. You can make multiple selections. They get listed in sequential order.
Favorite Athletes	Enter the names of your favorite athletes. Facebook gives you choices as you type in the entry. You can either select your choice or type your text. You can make multiple selections. They get listed in sequential order.
Save Changes	Saves your entries.

> **Activities and Interests**

You can select the activities and interests and add them to your profile. If pages exist for the activities or interest you add, then you can link to them or make your own entry.

The following table provides more information on fields:

This Field	Requires...
Activities	Enter an activity you like to do. Facebook gives you choices as you type in the entry. You can either select your choice or type your text. You can make multiple entries. The fields "With" and "Description" get populated when you choose an activity.
With	Enter the details about your activity. Entry in "With" is associated with the activity.
Description	Any additional information or detail you want to enter about the activity.
Add activity	Saves the activity to your profile.
Cancel	Cancels the activity name and details.
Interests	Enter your interests. Facebook gives you choices as you type in the entry. You can either select your choice or type your text. You can make multiple entries.
Save Changes	Saves your entries.

➢ **Contact Information**

You can add, delete, or edit your contact information details as seen by others on Facebook. Previously filled in entries get populated.

The following table provides more information on fields:

This Field	Requires...
Emails	Your existing email address gets populated.
Add/Remove Emails	The control goes to the "Account" page where you can change the email address.
IM Screen Names	You can enter the screen names that you use in various chat applications. Select the screen name and the chat software. You can have multiple entries for screen names with respective chat applications.
Phones	Select from "Work," "Home," or "Mobile." Enter the number and select the country from the drop-down menu.
Add Another Phone	This lets you add another phone number entry.
Address	Enter your address.
City/Town	Enter your city/town.
Zip	Enter your zip code.
Neighborhood	Enter your neighborhood.
Website	You can enter your website name, address, and other details.
Save Changes	Saves your entries.

➢ **Add/Remove Emails**

You can change your email address for Facebook messages and notifications.

The following table provides more information on fields:

This Field	Requires...
New Contact Email	Enter your new email address.
Add New Email	A pop-up window comes confirming your Facebook password. Once confirmed, an email is sent to the verified and changed email address for activation.

Congratulations! Your Facebook account has been created, and your Facebook profile is complete! You can now begin adding friends, family, coworkers, and business associates.

See the end section of this book entitled "Integrating Social Media" for ideas on how to integrate your Facebook profile with your other social media profiles that are outlined in this book.

TWITTER

Twitter – An Introduction

Twitter is one of the world's largest and busiest social media and "micro-blogging" communities, with more than 200 million international users sharing over 155 million, short, 140-character-long 'tweet' messages daily. Tweets are sent and received either on the computer or a user's mobile phone. Your tweets could be a quick status update, business news, or any other information.

Twitter gives individuals, professionals, and businesses a way to build and interact with a wide audience, as their tweets are read and often shared with others. The Twitter platform is now an established part of the business world, with companies and recruiters actively participating; and regularly searching the community for professionals and expertise.

Other Twitter users "follow" your profile to subscribe to your public messages, which then appear not only on your profile page, but also in their streaming feed of tweets from all accounts that they have subscribed to. In turn, as you subscribe to follow other Twitter accounts, you expand your own network, with that user's tweets now appearing on your Twitter home page to read, with their latest messages appearing first.

As of mid-2011, 61 percent of tweets are in English, but a multitude of languages and countries can be found on Twitter. It's a business-friendly international community and audience, with a slightly older demographic than Facebook, which means you'll reach adult consumers.

- 45% of users are 18-34
- 24% are between 35-49
- 14% are over 50
- 14% are under 17

Twitter allows you to do the following:

- ❖ **Tweet.**
  This is a 140-character long message that you can send or receive. It could be a quick status update, business news, or any other information.

- ❖ **Follow other twitter users.**
  Search and follow your friends on Twitter. If your friend's profile is public, you will immediately start receiving their tweets on your home page. Otherwise, your friend will need to approve you before you start receiving their updates.

- ❖ **Follow your interests.**
  You can use Twitter to stay connected with the topics of your interests like art, entertainment, music, etc. You can find the public streams associated with your topics of interests and follow the conversation.

- ❖ **Use twitter for your business**.
  You can use Twitter to quickly share the latest happenings about your products and services with the people who are interested in them.

The tweets that you send are publicly visible by default, although you can restrict its visibility so that it is visible only to your followers. Your tweets are displayed on your profile page and on the home page of each of your followers. You can follow other users (i.e., you can subscribe to other user's tweets). That user's tweets will appear in your Twitter home page in reverse chronological order.

Twitter describes itself as a "real-time information network" that connects you with new information that interests you—"the best way to discover what's new in your world" for the following reasons:

- You don't have to be active or even tweet to participate. You can follow conversations and access information and news as it happens in real-time in your areas of interest.

- If you're a business owner, Twitter connects you to customers in real-time, enabling you to share information about your products and services with your followers; follow market news and discussions; and build relationships with an engaged audience.

As you start to develop your profile and learn how to grow your Twitter audience, you can steadily expand your follower base. You will also gain benefits from the search engine tracking of keywords in your tweets.

Best Practices and Tips for Using Twitter

Twitter provides a constantly-expanding set of tactics for you and/or your business to leverage and work with. You can connect with new audiences by promoting campaigns, events, specials, and business news. Or simply study what others in your sector are doing and are interested in, and you can learn from their professional activity.

Get the most out of Twitter by following these best practices on what to say and how to grow your network:

- Just start tweeting. (Remember that everything you say is public!) People will follow if you have interesting and relevant things to say and if your Twitter profile is not too aggressively promotional.

- Before you seriously start building followers, you need to have at least 10-20 tweets in place so that new visitors will see something when they first land on your profile.

- As a general rule, tweet about things that are relevant to your area of expertise. You can mix in some personal items or general news or current events, but focus on building out your personal brand.

- Don't make too many tweets purely promotional and about yourself.

- Remember that this is a social community; interact, join in, and follow others in your industry and areas of interest. Get a good understanding of how the community works and learn from other profiles and what others in your field of expertise are doing.

What should you tweet?

Some suggestions to help you get started are the following:

- Relevant industry or online news
- Updates on your business and products/services
- Alerts on company or industry events
- Re-tweets of your followers' tweets
- Interesting URLs/links
- What you're reading online (e.g., a blog post, news article, or white paper that shows you're up to date with your industry)
- What you're watching, such as a YouTube video
- Replies to direct comments or questions
- Responses and participation comments in conversations with other users who interact with your profile
- Questions to get real-time feedback

Don't forget to listen! Monitor and respond to comments about your business or sector, regardless of whether they are positive or negative.

How Often and When Should You Tweet?

Tweet as much as you can! Even 1-3 daily tweets are a good start. The following are some tips and facts to remember:

- "Quality over quantity" should be your Twitter strategy. Post tweets when you have something good to share. There is a lot of spam and direct marketing messages on Twitter; avoid being part of this problem.

- With more than 155 million tweets going out daily, make your messages credible and informative to stand out as strongly as possible in your professional area.

- Be efficient. Get into a regular routine that works for you within your working day. Perhaps quickly adding updates through the day (45 seconds – 3 minutes), or limiting time to one or two 15 minute sessions a day or every other day.

- If you'd prefer to outsource your tweets, use scheduling services to automate and rotate regular messages. Some services can be found here:

  - **SocialOomph.com** (limited free version, scalable costs) is one leading service that sets up automated timed delivery of your regular promotional tweets, leaving you free to add fresh and timely new material.

  - **Hootsuite.com** is another leading third-party platform for scheduling and managing your tweets and Twitter activity, offering a free membership option.

How to Start Getting Followers

Getting started on building followers requires some initial work on your part. There are both unpaid ("organic") growth strategies and paid tactics and services to start audience-building.

The following are some tips to get you started:

- **Be genuine.**
  The best way to build followers on Twitter or any social medium is to be genuine, while having conversations and exchanges with your followers and contributing interesting information and input that others will want to read—and ideally share with others.

- **Follow first.**
  Find a set of potential followers and follow them first. This will encourage them to reciprocate, growing your initial follower count as a starting point. How? In "organic" growth strategies, start with Twitter's Search facility. Type in names and words - follow the profiles that you wish to. Repeat regularly over the days and weeks. A number of these people will follow you back.

Who should you not follow?

It's up to you whether you want to accept the system's initial suggestions of people you might want to follow, who tend to be celebrities, media and organizations. Although this is fun to do and gets you started, they will seldom follow you back, so your following/follower ratios will be distorted. Remember that whoever you follow, all their stream of tweets now appear on (and start to clog up) your page.

Avoid spam, network marketers, and porn accounts, unless you want their tweets all over your page, putting off potential valid followers. Let them follow you if you want to (for popularity purposes—people do like to follow profiles with lots of followers) unless you find them offensive, but don't return the favor.

Following Your Followers

Unless you object to any individual followers (simply delete or block inappropriate profiles— e.g., network or adult marketers), it is Twitter practice to follow at least some profiles who follow you. If you barely follow anyone, Twitter sets an upper limit on how fast you can grow your follower base.

As you find profiles where there's a strong overlap in content/target audiences, go into either or both their Following and Followers lists. As time, patience and determination permits, skim those lists quickly checking for people and organizations that you also want to follow.

You'll note that there are almost always less people in "Following" lists than "followers." This is useful to you because it points you quickly to other profiles that the user has deemed influential, interesting, useful, or relevant enough to follow.

People Who You Are Now Following

Not everyone that you follow will follow you back. Some approximately 30-50% of people will usually reciprocate, to help initially build your list. Regularly check the list of people that you follow, which shows on your profile page.

If your Following/Followers numbers are markedly different, Twitter's rules will block you from adding new followers until you delete some of the profiles that you've followed (until you have over 2,000 followers).

Check in at least twice weekly to make decisions about whether or not to leave certain profiles on your Following tab. Delete followers who don't follow back in order to make space for those who will.

Some exceptions are profiles that you want to track, such as profiles with big or useful lists where you can find local/regional followers, or competitors that you want to benchmark against.

Twitter Lists

On your main home page, you will see the List function. This is a very useful tool, creating new databases for your networking.

So give some thought to the lists that you set up right from the beginning. Perhaps you don't think that you need this function. We recommend using Lists from the outset, as it is much easier to add new followers to lists as they join up, rather than later trying to go through your entire database and doing this.

Other Twitter users will gradually start to add you to their own lists, in turn helping you to be found by people visiting those profiles/lists and noting who they've listed.

Resources and Tools

- **Mashable.com**
  This site has excellent updates/tips on effectively utilizing Twitter: http://mashable.com/category/twitter-lists/. Check regularly and/or subscribe to their daily news feed.

- **TechCrunch.com's**
  Subscribe to their daily bulletin.

- **www.Tweetdeck.com**
  This site has a desktop application for daily use, the #1 Twitter Application for ease of use in administering your account, posting, shortening URLs, tracking replies and direct messages, etc.

- **www.SeesmicDesktop and www.Hootsuite.com**
  These are two other leading software platforms.

- **www.TwitThat.com**

49

This site has a browser plug-in—you can post interesting things with one click.

- **www.SocialOomph.com**
  This site allows you to schedule tweets for later/regular delivery.

How to Set Up a Twitter Account

This section of the book explains the procedure to open a Twitter account, complete your Twitter profile, and follow your friends and interests.

➢ Registration

To create a profile and build a professional network, you have to open an account with Twitter which is absolutely free. The Twitter registration process is described below.

➢ Getting Started

Open a new browser window. You can use any browser like Internet Explorer, Chrome, or Firefox etc. I am using Firefox here. Enter the URL www.twitter.com in the browser address bar and press **Enter**.

The Twitter Home Page is displayed as shown below.

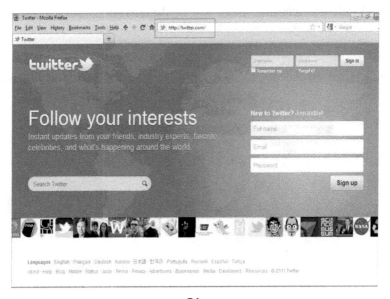

➢ Join Now

To start the registration process, fill in the information under "New to Twitter? Join today!"

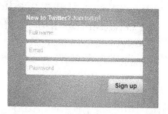

Complete the entries in the fields. The following table provides more information:

This Field	Requires...
Full name	Enter your full name. This name may become your username if it is available.
Email	Enter your email address.
Password	Enter your password.
Sign up	Click the **Sign up** button.

The "Create an Account" page will be displayed.

➢ Create an Account

The "Create an Account" page enables you to start building your profile.

Complete the entries in the fields. The following table provides more information:

This Field	Contains/Requires...
Full Name	Your full name that you entered on the "Join Now" page is displayed. Suggestion about the name is also displayed.
Email	Your Email that you entered on the "Join Now" page is displayed. You will receive a confirmation email from Twitter in regards to this email ID.
Password	Your password that you entered on the "Join Now" page is displayed. Password strength and suggestion about the password are also displayed.
Username	Your full name becomes your username if it is available. If it is not available, a suggested username is displayed. More suggestions for username are also displayed. You can edit the username and check its availability.
Create my account	Click the **Create my account** button.

The "Who to Follow/Interests" page will be displayed.

> **Who to Follow/Interests**

You can select topics or groups that you are interested in, or you can find a few people you want to hear from and follow them. You can get instant updates from industry experts and/or favorite celebrities by following them.

Before you proceed to the next step of the registration process, you are encouraged to start following at least 10 users that are of interest to you so that you can get the most out of Twitter.

The "Who to Follow/Interests" page is shown below.

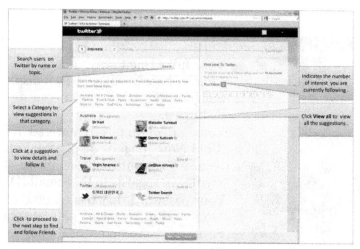

You can search users on Twitter by name or topic. You can select a category or click **View all** to view all the suggestions in that category. You can click a suggestion to view its details and follow it. You can also skip this step and proceed to the next step of finding and following friends.

After selecting a category you can view all the interests in a category as shown in the figure below.

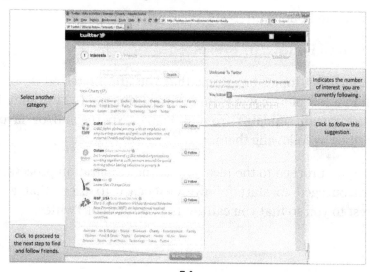

You can follow one or more interests by clicking on the **Follow** button. The **Follow** button turns green to depict that you are currently following it as shown in the figure below.

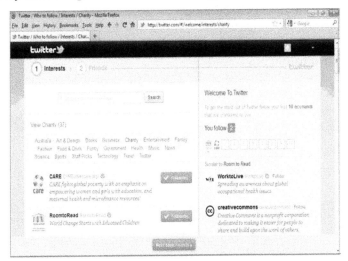

If you do not want to follow the interest that you are currently following, you can "Unfollow." To do so, move the mouse pointer over the green **Following** button. It will turn into red **Unfollow** button. Click it to mark the interest as "Unfollow" as shown in the figure below.

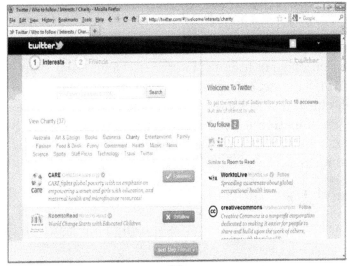

Repeat the above mentioned steps to follow more interests. You are encouraged to follow 10 interests, although you can follow as many interests as you want. You can also do it later after your Twitter profile has been created.

Click the **Next Step: Friends** button to move to the next step of finding and following friends.

➢ **Who to Follow/Find Friends**

The "Who to Follow/Find Friends" page is displayed below:

You can enter your friend's Twitter username and search for it. You can also import contacts from your email accounts like Gmail, Yahoo!, etc. and start following them on Twitter. You can go back to the previous step to follow more interests by clicking **Back to Interests** button. If you want, you can also skip this step and proceed further by clicking **Skip Import** button.

➢ **Search Users on Twitter**

You can search users on Twitter as shown in the figure on the next page.

Enter your friend's Twitter username and click **Search**. The matching Twitter users are displayed. If your friend's profile is displayed, click **Follow**; otherwise, search again.

➢ **Search Contacts in Your Email Account**

You can import contacts from any of your email accounts like Gmail, Yahoo!, etc. If these contacts are existing Twitter users, you can start following them; otherwise, you can invite them to Twitter.

After choosing an email account, you will be directed to log in securely using the login details of that email account. You will also have to authorize Twitter to access your contacts.

The process of importing contacts from LinkedIn and Gmail are discussed below. You can import contacts from other email accounts in the same way.

➢ **Import Contacts from LinkedIn**

Click the **Search Contacts** button to import contacts from your LinkedIn account as shown in the figure below.

The "Sign in to LinkedIn" page is displayed in a new window as shown in the figure on the next page.

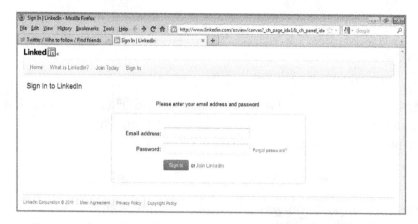

Complete the entries in the fields. The following table provides more information.

This Field	Requires...
Email address	Enter the email address that is previously registered with LinkedIn.
Password	Enter your LinkedIn password.
Sign In	Click **Sign In**.

The "Security Verification" page will be displayed as shown below.

Enter the text as displayed in the CAPTCHA image, and click **Continue**.

Your LinkedIn contacts are displayed as shown in the figure below.

Click **Follow** to follow one or more contacts on Twitter. The **Follow** button turns into **Unfollow** for the contacts you are currently following as shown in the figure below.

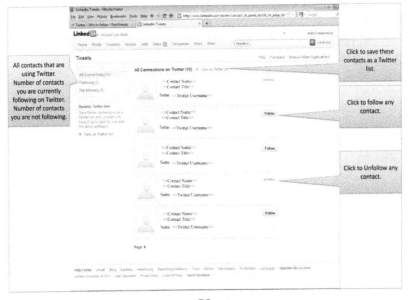

You will start receiving tweets from the friends you are currently "Following."

➢ **Import Contacts from Gmail**

Click the **Search contacts** button to import contacts from your Gmail account as shown in the figure below.

The "Google Accounts" pop-up window is displayed, where you can sign in as displayed in the figure below.

Complete the entries in the fields. The following table on the next page provides more information:

This Field	Requires...
Email	Enter your email address for Gmail.
Password	Enter your Gmail password.
Sign In	Click **Sign In**.

The "My Account" page is displayed as shown in the figure below.

Click the **Grant access** button to allow Twitter to access your Google Contacts. The list of contacts using Twitter is displayed as shown in the figure below.

All the contacts that are already using Twitter are displayed. You can invite the others to Twitter.

Click the **Try another service** link to search contacts in other accounts. Click **Back to interests** to go back to the previous step of interests.

Click the **Follow All** button to start following all the contacts; otherwise, click the **Follow** button to follow any contact. The **Follow** button turns green into the **Following** button as shown in the figure below.

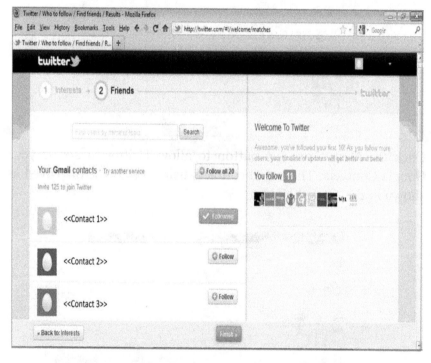

If you want to unfollow any contact, move the mouse pointer over the green **Following** button, and it will turn into a red **Unfollow** button. Click it to unfollow the contact as shown in the figure on the next page.

Click **Finish** once you are done with following the contacts. The "Invite your friends who aren't on Twitter" pop-up window is displayed as shown in the figure below.

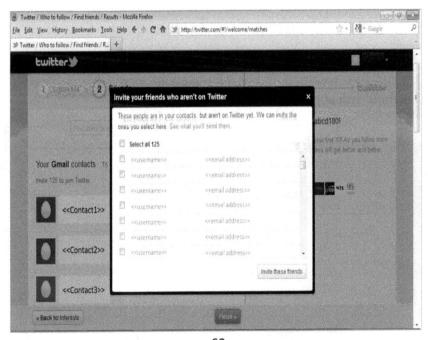

The list of friends who are not on Twitter is displayed. Select the check boxes of the friends you want to invite and click the **Invite these friends** button. These friends will receive the invite to join Twitter in their Gmail inbox.

The Twitter Home page is displayed with the message that a confirmation email has been sent to the email address with which you have registered in Twitter.

➤ **Confirm Your Email Address**

Twitter will perform email authentication to complete your registration. Twitter will send an email to your email address registered with Twitter. You will have to log in to your email and click on the confirmation link in the email to activate your account.

The "Confirm Your Email Address" page is shown below.

Confirm Your Email Address

A confirmation email has been sent to   your email   Click on the confirmation link in the email to activate your account.

Log into your webmail and check the email received from Twitter. The email will appear something like this:

Please confirm your Twitter account by clicking this link:
http://twitter.com/account/confirm_email/abcd180/GG7ED-896F7-130996

Once you confirm, you will have full access to Twitter and all future notifications will be sent to this email address.

The Twitter Team

If you received this message in error and did not sign up for a Twitter account, click not my account.

Please do not reply to this message; it was sent from an unmonitored email address. This message is a service email related to your use of Twitter. For general inquiries or to request support with your Twitter account, please visit us at Twitter Support

Click or paste the confirmation link in your browser's address bar, and the Twitter Home page will be displayed, which is shown below.

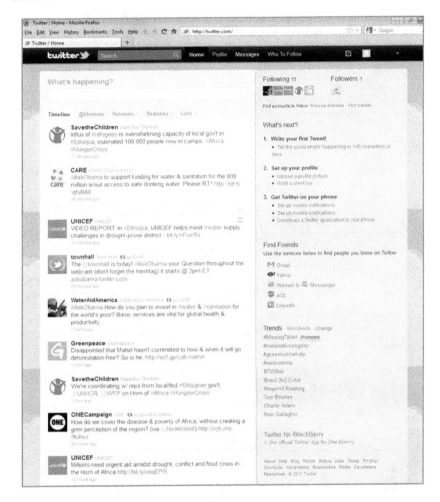

> **Build Your Twitter Profile**

Once your account is setup, you can start building your Twitter profile. The profile information you provide here will appear in your public profile. It will help those who are following you to identify you. It will also help your friends to search for you on Twitter.

Click the Profile tab in the header as shown in the figure below.

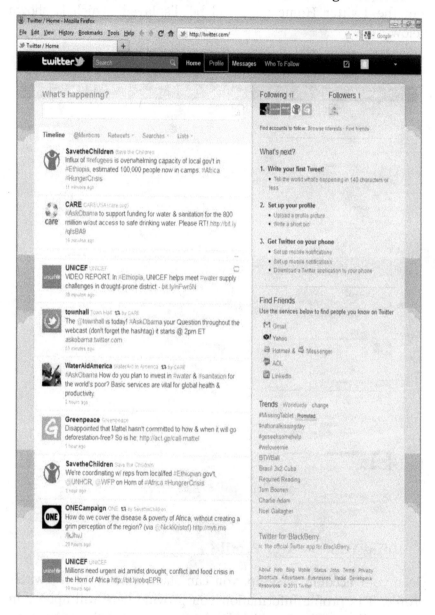

The Profile page is displayed as shown below.

Click the **Edit your profile** link to set up your profile.

The Edit Profile page is displayed as shown below.

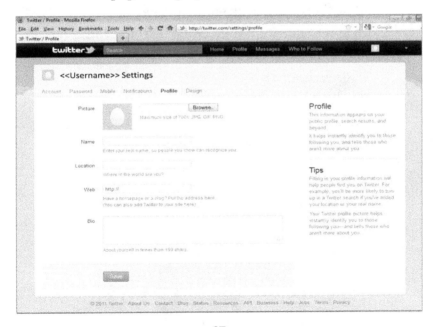

Complete the entries in the fields. The following table provides more information:

This Field	Requires...
Picture	Click the **Browse** button to locate and select your picture from your computer. The picture could be in JPG, GIF, or PNG format.
Name	Enter your real name to help your friends recognize you.
Location	Enter your location to help your friends search for you on Twitter.
Web	If you have a homepage or a blog site, enter its URL here.
Bio	Write your short bio to help people who are following you know you better.
Save	Click the **Save** button to save your profile information.

Congratulations! Your Twitter account is created, and your Twitter profile is set up. You are now ready to start tweeting.

See the end section of this book entitled "Integrating Social Media" for ideas on how to integrate your Twitter account with your other social media profiles that are outlined in this book.

LINKEDIN

LinkedIn – An Introduction

LinkedIn.com is the world's largest online business network, connecting you with more than 100 million professional members in over 200 countries.

The popular business site and community enables you to showcase your professional profile, highlighting your education, skills and experience and sharing testimonials from clients and previous employers.

Enhance your credibility and visibility by joining LinkedIn as a free member to network with your existing contacts, invite others to join and to connect to a wider business network of individuals and companies to share information, thoughts, and opportunities.

The LinkedIn professional community has highly engaged, active and well-qualified users. With an average age of 43, more than 77% have a university degree, and 32% are in mid-management or higher positions. Members are currently split evenly between North America and international locations, and they are 54% male and 46% female.

Your LinkedIn network is your connections, your connections' connections, and the people they know—potentially linking you to a huge number of qualified professionals and organizations.

LinkedIn allows you to accomplish the following:

❖ **Showcase Your Professional Profile**
Create a LinkedIn professional profile that showcases your education, skills, and experience. This profile will become your professional identity online.

❖ **Build Your Network**

Search, connect, communicate, and collaborate with your classmates, colleagues, friends, and other professionals. You can stay in touch with your connections and find out what is happening in their professional lives.

❖ **Join LinkedIn Groups**

Join a LinkedIn Group to connect with other professionals with similar interests. You can interact with experts and find out the knowledge you are looking for.

❖ **Create a Group**

If no one has created one already, create one! You will get more members in a new group for your industry, not just your company.

❖ **Explore Career Opportunities**

Search the jobs posted in LinkedIn, conduct a company research, and find connections inside the companies you want to work for.

❖ **Send and Receive Status Updates**

You can send status updates about your professional life to your connections and receive their status updates. You can also link your Twitter account so that your tweets are automatically shared with your connections.

❖ **Premium Benefits**

You can choose a Basic level or Premium level plan for your LinkedIn account. The Basic level plan allows you to avail most of the above mentioned benefits. With a Premium Level plan, you get extra benefits. For example, you can send messages to people you aren't directly connected to, use advanced search tools—like search alerts and filters—save profiles into folders, etc.

Best Practices and Tips for Using Linked In

Follow these best practice guidelines and expert tips to get the most out of LinkedIn:

- Ask or answer questions in your area of expertise. Answers are read widely by other members and give you exposure to new audiences; your answer can also be chosen as "best answer," highlighting that endorsement on your profile page.

- Fully fill out your Profile.

- Your Summary is indexed by search engines, so include keywords, your skills (tip: first search LinkedIn for skills to be able to add your own), experience, and professional selling points and specialties.

- Request and give recommendations.

- Upload a good professional-looking photo.

- Edit your public profile URL. Select your name if available and use this URL on your business cards, email signature file, and other marketing materials.

- Include links to your company website(s) and Facebook page/other sites.

- Promote yourself further through setting up automatic feeds from your Twitter profile and Blog featuring on the sidebars of your Profile.

- Build your creative Portfolio.

- Upload Slideshows and Presentations.

- Set up a Company Page for your organization or services.

- Upgrade to a professional membership to be able to send messages to people you are not directly connected to; use advanced search tools; save profiles into folders, etc.

- Explore career opportunities. Search jobs posted—find connections inside a company you want to work for.

- Post and distribute job listings.

- Publicize an event.

- Conduct short polls.

- Monitor who has viewed you and how often you show up in LinkedIn searches.

- Schedule LinkedIn updates for efficiency using a desktop application client like Tweetdeck.com, Hootsuite.com, or Seesmic.com.

- Tag a tweet to post on LinkedIn by adding "#in" to the tweet.

How to Use LinkedIn

Through your network, you can...

- Manage publicly available information about you;
- Find/be introduced to potential clients, providers, and experts;
- Be found for opportunities or find business partners;
- Have discussions with other professionals; and
- Discover inside connections to win business or successfully close deals.

The community is now an active part of the hiring and job-search process, with recruiters and HR professionals on LinkedIn seeking out top candidates and cross-referencing job-seekers. For consultants, contractors, and experts, it provides another online marketing channel to connect with new contacts and customers and for those businesses to check your credentials and approach.

How to Set Up a LinkedIn Account

This section of the book explains the procedure to open a LinkedIn account, complete your LinkedIn profile, and add connections.

➤ **Registration**

To create a profile and build a professional network, you have to open an account with LinkedIn, which is absolutely free. The LinkedIn registration process is described below.

➤ **Getting Started**

Open a new browser window. You can use any browser, like Internet Explorer, Chrome, Firefox, etc. I am using Firefox here. Enter the URL www.linkedin.com in the browser address bar and press **Enter**.

The LinkedIn Home Page is displayed as shown below.

➢ **Join Now**

To start the registration process, fill in the information under "Join LinkedIn Today."

Complete the entries in the fields. The following table provides more information:

This Field	Requires...
First Name	Enter your first name. Your first name and the last initial will be displayed in your profile as your username. Your connections will see your first and last name.
Last Name	Enter your last name.
Email	Enter your email address. This will be your primary email address. This is the address that you will log in with. LinkedIn will deliver all email messages regarding invitations, requests, and other system emails to this email address.
Password	Enter your password.
Join Now	Click the **Join Now** button.

The "Build Your Profile" page will be displayed.

> **Start Building Your Profile**

The "Build Your Profile" page enables you to start building your profile.

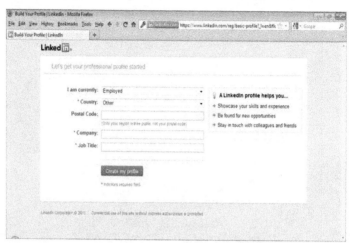

Complete the entries in the fields. The following table provides more information:

This Field	Requires...
I am currently	Open the drop-down box and select one of the following: "Employed," "A business owner," "Looking for work," "Working independently," or "A student."
Country	Open the drop-down box and select the country.
Postal Code	Enter your postal code.
Company	Enter your company name.
Job Title	Enter your job title. The job title and the company name will form the headline of your profile.
Create my profile	Click **Create my profile**.

The "Add Connections" page will be displayed.

> **Search Email Contacts**

You can allow LinkedIn to search your email contacts and find the people you already know on LinkedIn.

The "Add Connections" page is shown below.

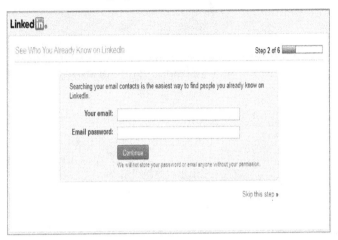

Complete the entries in the fields. The following table provides more information.

This Field	Requires...
Your Email	Enter your email address. This is the email address in which you want LinkedIn to search the contacts. This may or may not be the primary email address you provided previously for registration.
Email Password	Enter your email password for the above email address.
Continue	Click **Continue**.
Skip This Step	If you don't want to search for email contacts now, you can click **Skip this step** to move on to the next step.

LinkedIn will search your email contacts, and find and display the contacts that have a LinkedIn account. You can select contact(s) and add them as a connection.

77

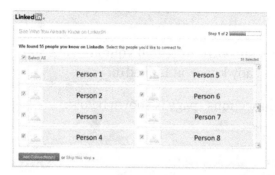

Complete the entries in the fields. The following table provides more information:

This Field	Requires...
Select Contact	Select the check box of the contact you want to add. You can select one or more contacts.
Select All	Click on the **Select All** check box if you want to add all the contacts.
Add Connection(s)	Click **Add Connection(s)**.
Skip this step	If you don't want to add connections now, you can click **Skip this step** to move to the next step.

After adding connections, you can invite those contacts to LinkedIn who don't have a LinkedIn account. The "Invite Contacts" page will be displayed, and it is shown below.

Complete the entries in the fields. The following table provides more information:

This Field	Requires...
Select Contact	Select the check box of the contact you want to invite. You can select one or more contacts.
Select All	Click on the **Select All** check box if you want to invite all the contacts.
Add Connection(s)	Click **Invite to Connect**.
Skip this step	If you don't want to invite contacts now, you can click **Skip This Step** to move to the next step.

The "Confirm Your Email Address" page will be displayed.

> **Confirm Your Email Address**

LinkedIn will perform email authentication to complete your registration. LinkedIn will send an email to your primary email address. You will have to log into your email and click on the confirmation link in the email to activate your account.

The "Confirm Your Email Address" page is shown below.

Confirm Your Email Address

A confirmation email has been sent to your email. Click on the confirmation link in the email to activate your account.

Log into your webmail and check the email received from LinkedIn. The email will appear something like this:

LinkedIn

Click here to confirm your email address.

If the above link does not work, you can paste the following address into your browser:

https://www.linkedin.com/e/csrfXdlx/-8dlcbi-gnwrvl0j-55/cnf/B0A-rP-IXrDO-48V-Ptw/

You will be asked to log into your account to confirm this email address. Be sure to log in with your current primary email address.

We ask you to confirm your email address before sending invitations or requesting contacts at LinkedIn. You can have several email addresses, but one will need to be confirmed at all times to use the system.

If you have more than one email address, you can choose one to be your **primary email address**. This is the address you will log in with, and the address to which we will deliver all email messages regarding invitations and requests, and other system mail.

Thank you for using LinkedIn!

--The LinkedIn Team
http://www.linkedin.com/

© 2011, LinkedIn Corporation

Click or paste the confirmation link in your browser's address bar. The "Confirm Your Email Address" page will display and is shown below.

Click the **Confirm** button. You will be asked to sign in to your account to confirm your email address.

➢ **Sign In**

After your account is created you will have to sign in whenever you access your LinkedIn account.

If you were invited to join LinkedIn, you can directly sign in using the email address at which you were invited. Signing in will automatically add the person who invited you to your LinkedIn account.

The "Sign In" page is shown below.

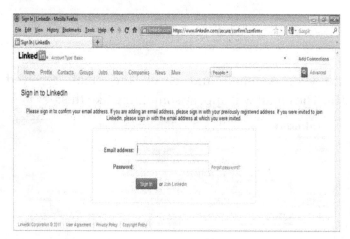

Complete the entries in the fields. The following table provides more information.

This Field	Requires...
Email address	Enter your previously registered primary email address or the email at which you were invited.
Password	Enter your password.
Sign In	Click **Sign In**.

The "Suggested Connections" page will be displayed.

➢ **Suggested Connections**

LinkedIn suggests connections for you based on your primary email address. The "Suggested Connections" page is displayed below.

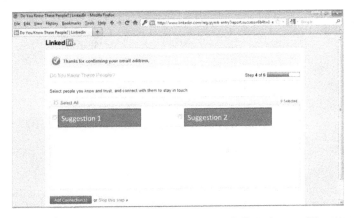

Complete the entries in the fields. The following table provides more information.

This Field	Requires...
Select Connection	Select the check box of the connection you want to add. You can select one or more connections.
Select All	Click on the **Select All** check box if you want to add all the connections.
Add Connection(s)	Click **Add Connection(s)**.
Skip this step	If you don't want to add connections now, you can click **Skip this step** to move to the next step.

The "Create Invitations" page will be displayed.

➢ Create Invitations

You can invite your friends to LinkedIn so that you can add them as connection. The "Create Invitations" page is displayed below.

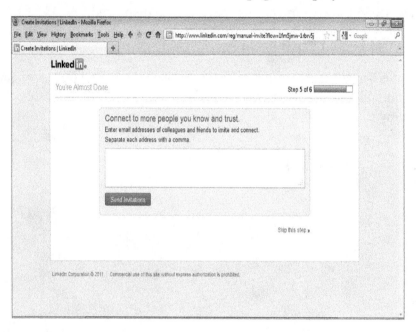

Complete the entries in the fields. The following table provides more information:

This Field	Requires...
Enter Email Addresses	Enter the email addresses of your friends. Separate each address with a comma.
Send Invitations	Click the **Send Invitations** button.
Skip this step	If you don't want to create invitations now, you can click **Skip this step** to move to the next step.

The "Choose Your Plan Level" page will be displayed.

➢ **Choose Your Plan Level**

You can choose the Basic or Premium plan level. The Basic plan level is free. You will have to pay for the Premium plan level, which gives you extra benefits.

The "Choose Your Plan Level" page is shown below.

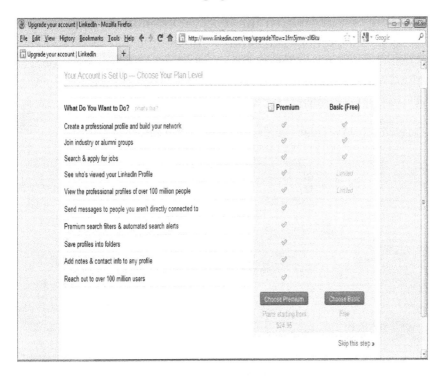

Complete the entries in the fields. The following table provides more information:

This Field	Requires...
Choose Plan Level	Choose the plan level and click on the **Choose Premium** or **Choose Basic** button.
Skip this step	If you don't want to choose a plan level now, you can click **Skip this step** to move to the next step.

If you selected the Premium plan level, you will be taken to the "Make Payment" page. After you successfully make the payment, the "Home" page is displayed.

If you selected the Basic level, the "Home" page is displayed.

> **Build Profile**

After you have completed the registration process, you can start building your professional profile. This profile will showcase your education, skills, and experience, and it will be your identity online. If you have a complete profile, you are more likely to receive opportunities through LinkedIn.

Move the mouse over the Profile tab and click **Edit Profile**.

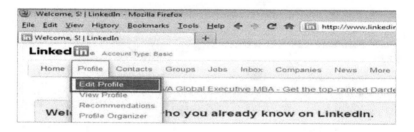

The "Edit Profile" page is displayed.

➢ Add Current Position

Enter the details about your current position. Click the **Add a current position** link under "Current" in the Edit Profile page.

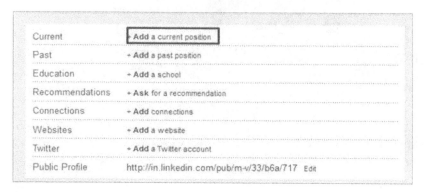

The "Add Position" page is displayed.

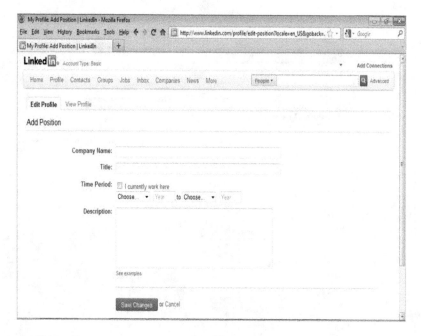

Complete the entries in the fields. The following table provides more information:

This Field	Requires...
Company Name	Enter the company name. As you start entering the company name, already existing companies are shown as suggestions. Click on a company name to select one of them or else enter a new company name. If you have entered a new company name, you will be asked to enter more information about this company, like the website and industry information.
Title	Enter the title.
Time Period	If this is your current position, select the "I currently work here" check box. You only need to select the "from" year. If you do not select the "I currently work here" check box, you need to select the "from" date and "to" date. To select a date, select the month and enter the year in "yyyy" format. If you are adding this as your current position, your title and company name will be added in the Headline.
Headline	If you want to edit the Headline, select the "Update my headline to" check box. You can now edit the Headline.
Description	Enter your position description. Click "See examples" link to see some examples of the "Description."
Update/Cancel	Click **Update** to add this position to your profile or click the **Cancel button** to cancel adding the position and go back to the "Edit Profile" page.

The position is added, and the "Edit Profile" page is displayed.

➢ **Add a Past Position**

Enter the details about your past position. Click **Add a past position** link under "Past" in the Edit profile page.

Current	+ Add a current position
Past	+ Add a past position
Education	+ Add a school
Recommendations	+ Ask for a recommendation
Connections	+ Add connections
Websites	+ Add a website
Twitter	+ Add a Twitter account
Public Profile	http://in.linkedin.com/pub/m-v/33/b6a/717 Edit

The "Add Position" page is displayed.

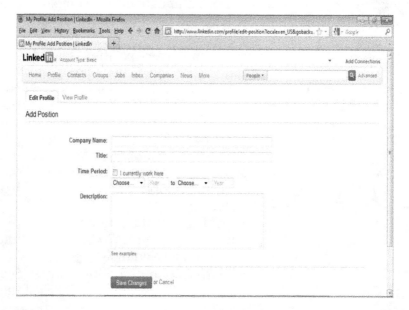

Complete the entries in the fields. The following table provides more information:

This Field	Requires...
Company Name	Enter the company name. As you start entering the company name, already existing companies are shown as suggestions. Click on a company name to select one of them; otherwise, enter a new company name. If you have entered a new company name, you will be asked to enter more information about this company, like website and industry information.

88

This Field	Requires...
Title	Enter the title.
Time Period	If this is your past position, do not select the "I currently work here" check box. Enter the "from" date and "to" date. To select a date, select the month and enter the year in "yyyy" format.
Description	Enter your position description. Click the **See examples** link to see some examples of the "Description."
Update/Cancel	Click **Update** to add this position to your profile, or click **Cancel** to cancel adding the position and go back to the "Edit Profile" page.

The position is added, and the "Edit Profile" page will be displayed.

➢ **Add Education**

Enter the details about your education. Click the **Add a school** link under "Education" in the "Edit Profile" page.

The "Add Education" page will be displayed.

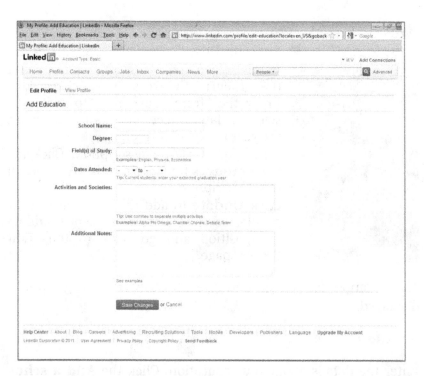

Complete the entries in the fields. The following table provides more information:

This Field	Requires...
School Name	Enter the name of your school.
Degree	Enter your degree.
Field(s) of Study	Enter the field(s) of study, for example English, Physics, Economics, etc.
Dates Attended	Select the "from" year and "to" year.
Activities and Societies	Enter comma separated activities and societies.
Additional Notes	Enter additional educational description. Click "See examples" to see the examples of additional notes.
Save Changes/Cancel	Click **Save Changes** to save the educational details, or click **Cancel** to cancel adding the education and go back to the "Edit Profile" page.

The education is added, and the "Edit Profile" page is displayed.

> **Add Profile Summary & Specialities**

The profile summary should be a description of your job and your past experiences.

Click **Add Summary** link under "Summary" in the Edit Profile page.

The "Professional Summary" page will be displayed.

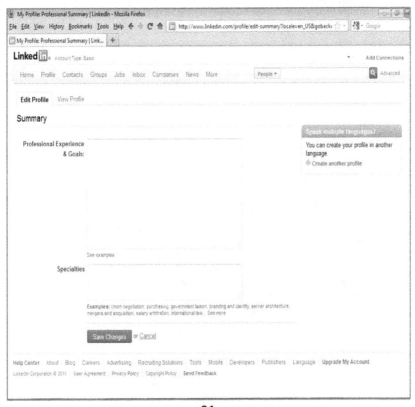

Complete the entries in the fields. The following table provides more information:

This Field	Requires...
Professional Experience & Goals	Enter your professional experience and goals. If you need help, click "See examples" to see the examples of professional experience and goals.
Specialities	Enter your specialities, i.e., the special fields of union negotiation, purchasing, etc., in which you have experience.
Save Changes/Cancel	Click **Save Changes** to save the summary, or click **Cancel** to cancel adding the summary and go back to the "Edit Profile" page.

The summary is added and the "Edit Profile" page is displayed.

➢ **Add Profile Photo**

Add a profile photo to make your profile look complete. Click the **Add Photo** link under the profile photo in the "Edit Profile" page.

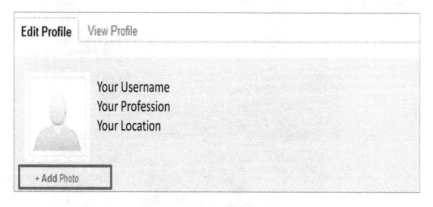

The "Add Photo" page will be displayed.

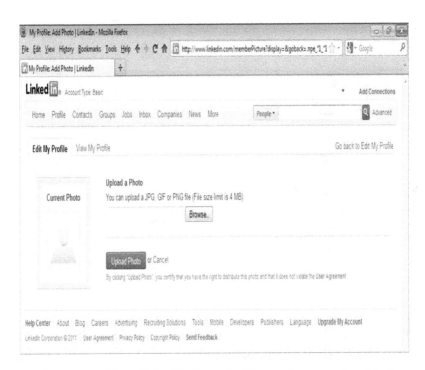

Your "Current Photo" is displayed. If you have not added any photo, the LinkedIn default profile photo is displayed. Click **Browse** to browse your computer and upload a photo in JPG, GIF, or PNG format. The file size is limited to 4 MB.

After selecting a file, click **Upload Photo**.

Click **Cancel** to cancel uploading the photo and go back to the "Edit Profile" page. After you have uploaded a photo, you can preview the photo, i.e., what your profile photo will look like. To make adjustments, you can drag around and resize a yellow square shown on the photo.

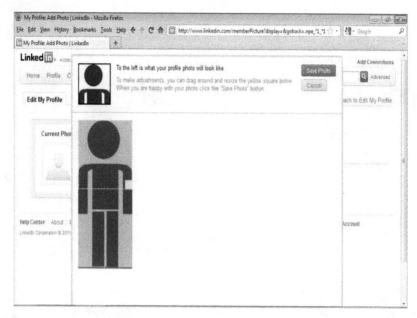

When you are happy with your photo, click the **Save Photo** button. If you want to cancel uploading the photo click the **Cancel** button.

The "Edit Profile" page will be displayed.

➤ **Ask for a Recommendation**

You can ask your colleagues or classmates to recommend you. These recommendations are displayed in your profile.

Click the **Ask for a recommendation** link under "Recommendations" in the "Edit Profile" page.

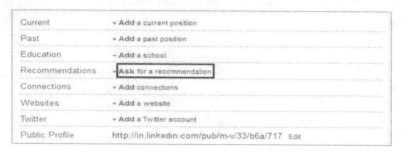

The "Request Recommendation" page will be displayed.

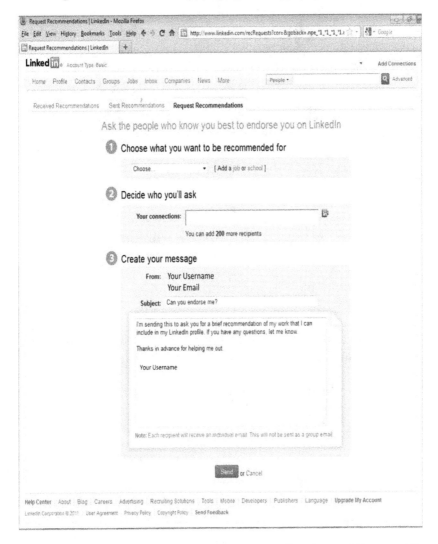

Complete the entries in the fields. The following table provides more information:

This Field	Requires...
Choose what you want to be	Choose a school or current or past job from the drop-down box for which you

This Field	Requires...
recommended for	want to be recommended. You can also add a school or job by clicking on the **Add a school or job** link.
Decide who you'll ask	Depending on your selection of school or job above, you can select a connection (classmate or colleague) whom you want to ask for recommendation.
Create your message	Enter a subject and your message.
Send/Cancel	Click **Send** to send your message, or click **Cancel** to cancel sending the message and go back to the "Edit Profile" page.

The message is sent to the recipient(s). The recipient(s) will write recommendations for you, which will be posted under "Recommendations" in your profile page.

The "Edit Profile" page is displayed.

1.1. Add Additional Information

You can add additional information in your profile about yourself and your profession.

Click **Add** to add any information.

The "Additional Information" page will be displayed.

Complete the entries in the fields. The following table provides more information:

This Field	Requires...
Websites	You can add up to 3 websites. Choose the type of website from the drop-down box like Personal Website, Company Website, Blog, RSS Feed, Portfolio, or Other. Enter the URL of the website—for example, www.site.com.
Interests	Enter your interests separated by commas—for example, investing, fishing, etc.

This Field	Requires...
Groups and Associations	Enter your groups and associations separated by commas—for example, IEEE, GNIIT, etc.
Honors and Awards	Enter your honors and awards, each separated by a comma.
Save Changes/Cancel	Click **Save Changes** to save the information, or click **Cancel** to cancel adding additional information and go back to the "Edit Profile" page.

The additional information is displayed in the "Edit Profile" page.

➢ **Add Personal Information**

You can add personal information in your profile about yourself.

Click **Add** for adding any information.

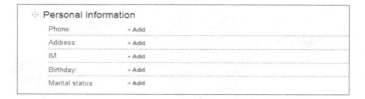

The "Personal Information" page will be displayed.

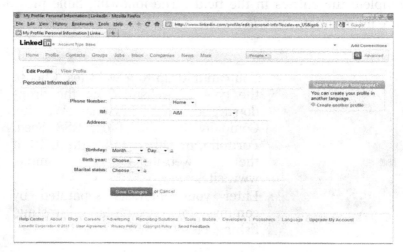

Complete the entries in the fields. The following table provides more information:

This Field	Requires...
Phone Number	Choose Home, Work, or Mobile from the drop-down box and enter your phone number.
IM	Select from AIM, Skype, Windows Live, Messenger, Yahoo! Messenger, ICQ, or GTalk, and enter your username.
Address	Enter your address.
Birthday	Enter the month and date of your birthday.
Birth year	Select your birth year.
Marital status	Choose Married or Single from the drop-down box.
Visibility Settings	For Birthday, Birth year, and Marital status fields, you can select the visibility settings by clicking on the visibility settings icon: 🔒 . You can make the fields visible to My Connections, My Network, or Everyone.
Save Changes/Cancel	Click **Save Changes** to save the information or click **Cancel** to cancel adding personal information and go back to the "Edit Profile" page.

The personal information is displayed in the "Edit Profile" page.

➢ **Contact Settings**

The "Contact Settings" page informs the users who view your profile about the types of contact you are interested in.

Click the **Edit** link under "Contact Settings" in the "Edit Profile" page.

The "Contact Settings" page will be displayed.

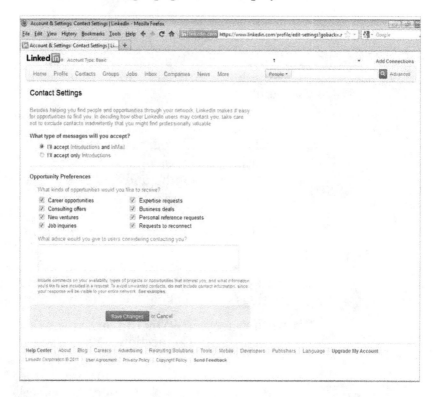

Complete the entries in the fields. The following table provides more information:

This Field	Requires...
What type of messages will you accept?	You can choose to accept Introductions and InMail or only Introductions. If you accept only Introductions, users not directly connected to you will be able to request an introduction through one of your connections. If you accept InMail, users not directly connected to you will be able to send you private messages about business and career opportunities.
Opportunity Preferences	You can select what kind of opportunities you would like to receive.

This Field	Requires...
What advice would you give to users considering contacting you?	Include comments on your availability, types of projects or opportunities that interest you, and what information you'd like to see included in a request. Click **See Examples** to view examples about writing this section.
Save Changes/Cancel	Click **Save Changes** to save the information, or click **Cancel** to cancel editing contact settings and go back to the "Edit Profile" page.

The contact settings you just made are displayed in the "Edit Profile" page.

> **Import Your Resume**

You can quickly complete your profile by importing your resume.

Click **Import Your Resume** in the "Edit Profile" page.

A pop-up window is displayed as shown below:

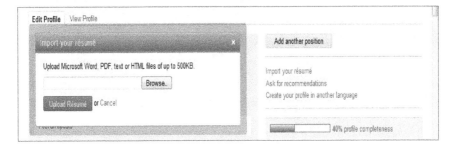

Browse your computer and select your resume in Microsoft Word, PDF, text, or HTML format. The file size is limited to 500 KB.

Click **Upload Resume**.

The information is imported from your resume and the Experience and Education sections are filled up automatically. The "Review Experience & Education" page is displayed where you can review the information and edit information if required.

Click **Save Changes** to save the information in your profile or click **Go Back to Edit Profile** to cancel saving information and move back to the "Edit Profile" page.

➤ **View Profile**

After editing the profile, you can see the public view of your profile by clicking the "View Profile" tab.

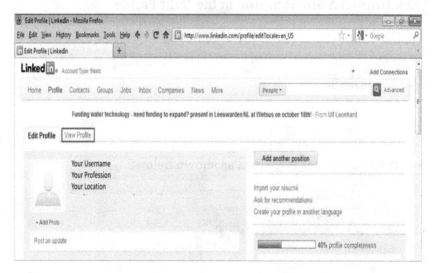

The public view of your profile will be displayed.

➢ **Manage Connections**

Connections are the people you want to associate yourself with in your professional network. You can add connections to your network during or after the registration process. You can find your trusted contacts on LinkedIn by searching your email contacts. After you add a connection, a request will be sent to that person, and they can either accept or decline your offer. If they accept, you are now connected to them and can see their full profile, and vice versa.

➢ **Add Connections**

Move the mouse over "Contacts" tab and click **Add Connections.**

The "Import Contacts and Invite" page will be displayed.

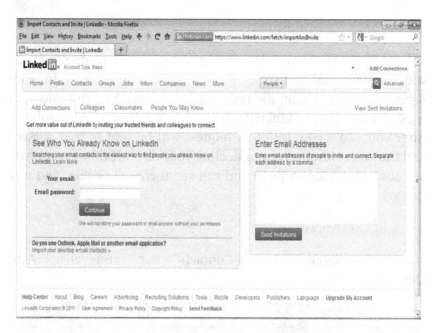

There are two methods to connect to the people you already know on LinkedIn. The first method is to allow LinkedIn to search your email contacts and display the ones who already have a LinkedIn account. The second method allows you to manually enter the email addresses of the persons you want to connect to.

For the first method, simply enter your email address and password and click **Continue.**

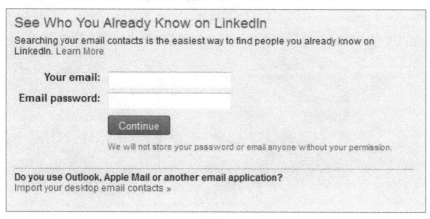

It will search and display a list of those contacts who have a LinkedIn account. Simply select the ones you want to connect and click the **Send Invitations** button.

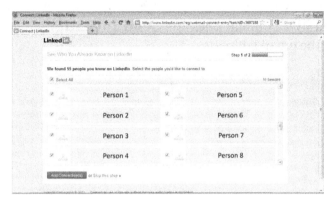

Connection request will be sent to the selected contacts. They can accept or decline your request. If they accept your request, they will be added to your "My Connections" list.

"Invite Contacts" page is displayed. It displays the list of your email contacts who don't have a LinkedIn account. If you want to connect with them on LinkedIn, you can invite them to join LinkedIn. To do this, simply select them and click **Invite to Connect**.

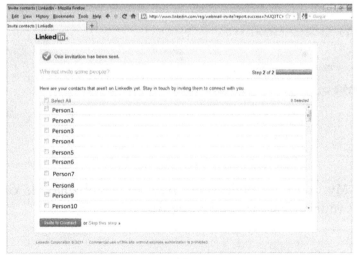

Invitations will be sent to the selected contacts to join LinkedIn.

The second method is to manually enter the email address of each person you wish to connect with. Each address should be separated by a comma. Click the **Send Invitations** button after entering the email addresses.

Invitations will be sent and the "Home" page will be displayed.

➢ **Add Colleagues**

You can find and connect to past or present colleagues.

Click on the "Colleagues" tab.

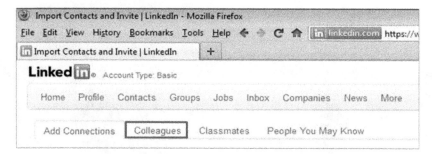

The "My Contacts: Colleagues" page will be displayed. You can search your present or past colleagues.

Click on **View all (present/past) colleagues**.

List of all the colleagues of the present/past company is displayed. Select the persons you want to connect to. Select the "Add a personal note with your invitation?" check box to attach a personal note with each invitation. Click **Send Invitations**.

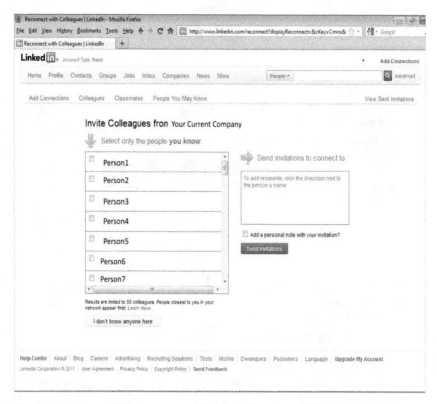

The invitation will be sent and "Home" page will be displayed.

➤ Add Classmates

You can add past or present classmates as connections on LinkedIn.

Click "Classmates" tab.

The "My Contacts: Classmates" page will be displayed.

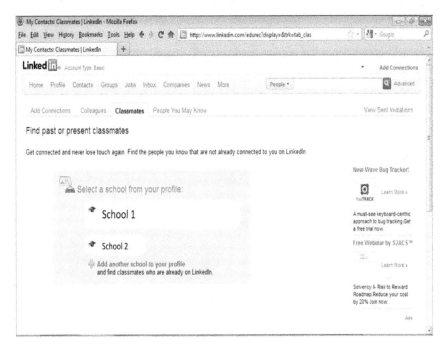

The schools added in your profile are displayed. Select one of the schools. The list of classmates from the selected school and year are displayed.

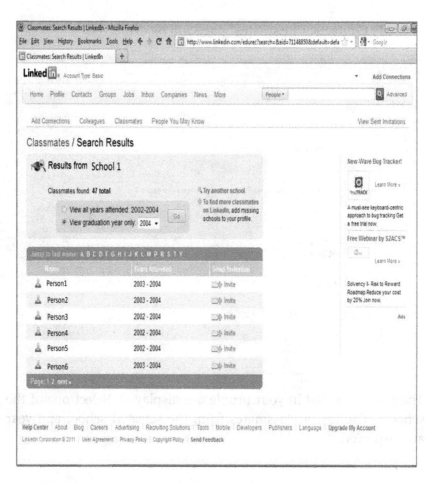

Click on the **Invite** button to send an invitation to a classmate. The invitation will be sent. Your classmates can accept or decline the invitation. If they accept your invitation, they will be added to your "My Connections" list.

Congratulations! Your LinkedIn account is now open!

See the end section of this book entitled "Integrating Social Media" for ideas on how to integrate your LinkedIn account with your other social media profiles that are outlined in this book.

TUMBLR

Tumblr – An Introduction

Tumblr is a social "micro-blogging" platform that has attracted 6.6 million users since its 2007 launch and is growing at a rate of 30,000 new users a day – and probably by now! Free and easy to use, Tumblr can be a cost effective and simple way for you to engage with customers, build long-term relationships, and extend your profile.

On Tumblr, like Facebook and Twitter, users share text, photos and videos that they find interesting, engaging with other users, who can view and follow your "tumblelogs" and share it with others.

After you open a Tumblr account, you can see which of your email contacts is already on the platform, following these people on Tumblr to get their updates. Find professional topics and areas of interest; then, follow users that are discussing these topics.

Setting up a Tumblr blog is simple and doesn't require any technical expertise on your part; you can be up and "tumbling" in just minutes. Everything can be customized on your profile, from your domain name, to choosing from hundreds of themes, and changing colors, fonts, and more.

Tumblr differs from Facebook and Twitter by being an open-ended platform, where users can share content and updates without any length or other restrictions.

Post what you'd like to, from wherever you are—at your computer, via mobile updates, or via email upload. You can use multi-media, such as audio, video, or slideshows; and there isn't a character or word limit for your postings.

The average user creates 14 original posts in a month, "reblogging" another 3 users' posts. 50 percent of these posts are images and photos, with the other 50 percent comprising text, music, video, links, and quotes.

Although Tumblr has considerably less users than Facebook or Twitter, brands that have established a presence have been able to share brand information with customers, build relationships, and drive traffic to their websites.

Tumblr allows you to do the following:

❖ **Post Anything**
You can post anything, like text, photos, audio, videos, links, slideshows, etc. that you create or find on the Internet.

❖ **Customize Blogs**
You can select from one of the several Tumblr themes or create your own theme for your blogs.

❖ **Choose a Domain Name**
You can choose a domain name for your blogs like <<yourname>>.tumblr.com and if it is available you can use it.

❖ **Make Your Blogs Private**
You can mark posts or blogs as private.

❖ **Follow Users**
You can follow other users and receive updates about their posts.

How Business People Are Using Tumblr

The following are some of the ways that business people are using Tumblr:

- Reblogging relevant and interesting user posts, just as users do on Twitter, Facebook, and YouTube

- Emailing or texting posts from their mobile phone

- Emailing posts that upload directly to their blog

- Sharing anything on the web by using the Tumblr Bookmarklet

- Using third party applications on Tumblr to further customize their content and profile

- Using the platform to boost SEO results, with Google optimizing search-friendly Tumblr features, from URLs to sitemaps

- "Group blogging" by inviting any number of users to contribute to one Tumblr blog, and enabling followers to submit guest posts for you to approve.

- Leveraging copyright of their Tumblr blogs, with a number of blogs attracting book deals in the past three years.

Best Practices and Tips for Using Tumblr

Follow these 2011 best practices to make the most of your professional presence on Tumblr:

- Get noticed by sharing great, exclusive, interesting content. Your Tumblr followers can re-post that on their own blogs, giving you valuable word-of-mouth exposure and the opportunity to benefit from that recommendation to another user's followers.

  Tip: don't cross-post the same material you're uploading to other social sites too often, use Tumblr to display different content and leverage its wide capabilities.

- Establish a voice and work towards being an influencer and expert on the system.

- Keep your posts short, include photos or videos.

114

- Curate and pass on content from external and industry sources—don't just post information on your own business.

- Interact! Follow other users and comment on their posts. Tumblr is an engaged community that needs energy and effort from you, and others won't engage with you until you initially make a first contact. Others will often follow you if you firstly follow them and also leave a comment.

- Reblog content that followers are posting, give your own perspective, or comment too on posts; show that you are active on the platform. Each post reblogged is potentially shown to multiple audiences, as you steadily grow your Tumblr network.

- Share your posts via auto-feeds to Facebook and Twitter and set up an RSS (Really Simple Syndication) feed for your blog.

- Use auto-scheduling tools to set up timed and staggered distribution of your content.

- Create a great theme for your Profile.

- Track your Tumblr statistics using Google Analytics.

- List your Tumblr blog in the official directory. You can ask your followers to recommend you for inclusion, or if you want to grow a large audience, paid inclusion is available as an option.

How to Set Up a Tumblr Account

This section of the book explains the procedure to open a Tumblr account, complete your Tumblr profile, and follow other users.

➢ **Registration**

To create a Tumblr account, you have to open an account with Tumblr, which is absolutely free. The Tumblr registration process is described below.

Open a new browser window. You can use any browser like Internet Explorer, Chrome, Firefox, etc. I am using Firefox here. Enter the URL www.tumblr.com in the browser address bar and press **Enter**.

The Tumblr "Log in" Page is displayed as shown below:

Complete the entries in the fields. The following table provides more information:

This Field	Requires...
Email Address	Enter your email address. This will become your login name. Tumblr will deliver all email messages regarding invitations, requests, and other system mails to this email address.
Password	Enter your password.
URL	Enter the URL for your blog site. For example, if you enter john, the URL will become http://john.tumblr.com. If the URL you have entered is not available, the error message: "This URL is already taken" appears. Enter another URL and check its availability. If it is available, it will become the URL of your blog site and users will be able to view your blogs at the URL http://john.tumblr.com.
Start Posting	Click the **Start Posting** button to sign up.

The security verification page is displayed. You have to enter the words displayed in the CAPTCHA picture into the textbox. You have the option to listen to audio and enter the words you hear. If the words are not clear, you can click the Refresh button to change the words.

The security verification page is displayed below:

Enter the text displayed and click the **I'm human!** button. The Tumblr dashboard is displayed.

➢ **Create Your First Post**

The Tumblr dashboard is displayed below.

Before the registration process is completed, you are encouraged to create your first post. You can try uploading a photo of yourself as your first post. Click the **Create your first post** link. The "Upload a Photo" page is displayed as shown below.

Complete the entries in the fields. The following table provides more information:

This Field	Requires...
Browse	Click the **Browse** button to locate and select a picture file in JPG, GIF, PNG, or BMP format.
Take a Photo	Click the **Take a Photo** button to instantly snap photo of yourself.

119

This Field	Requires...
Add Another Photo	If you want to upload more than one photo, click the **Add Another Photo** button.
Caption	If you want you can enter a caption for your photo, you can format the caption by using the various options like bold, italics, etc.
Use a URL instead	If your photo is already uploaded somewhere else, enter its URL here.
Set a click through link	If you want that when users click your photo they are taken to another page, enter that page's URL here.
Publish Now	Select one of the following options from the drop-down box: Publish Now, Add to Queue, Publish on, Save as Draft, or Private. Select the "Publish Now" option if you want the post to be published as soon as it is created. If you want the post to be added to queue, select the "Add to Queue" option. Select "Publish on" and specify a "Post Date," the post will be published on the specified date. If want to make changes later, save the post as draft by selecting the "Save as Draft" option. If you want to publish the post but don't want others to read it, mark the post as private by selecting the "Private" option.
Content Source	If you are using another web page for content, enter that page's URL here.
Tags	Enter tags to help the search engines like Google find your post.
Set a Custom Post URL	Create a custom URL for your post.
Let People Photo Reply	Select the check box to let people photo reply the post.
Create Post	Click the **Create Post** button to create the post. It will be published as per the settings done above.
Preview	Click **Preview** button to preview the post.
Cancel	Click **Cancel** to cancel creating the post.

The "Customize Your Blog" page will be displayed.

> **Customize Your Blog**

You can customize your blog page to give it a personal touch. You can apply various themes and apply formatting and style to your blog text.

The "Customize Your Blog" page is displayed below:

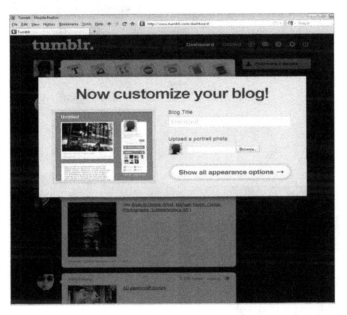

Complete the entries in the fields. The following table provides more information.

This Field	Requires...
Blog Title	Enter the blog title.
Upload a Portrait Photo	Click the **Browse** button to locate and select a photo from your computer.
Show All Appearance Options	To further customize your blog, click the **Show all appearance options.**

When you click **Show All Appearance Options** button, various options to customize the blogs are displayed as shown below:

> ➤ **Info**

The Info screen is displayed below.

Complete the entries in the fields. The following table provides more information.

This Field	Requires...
Title	The blog title you entered in the previous screen is displayed. If you want, you can edit it here.
Description	Enter the description for the blog.

➤ **Theme**

The theme screen is displayed below.

Select one of the themes for your blog. The themes are not free, and you will have to pay for it. Once you select a theme, you will be directed to the payment gateway to pay for it.

➢ **Appearance**

The appearance screen is displayed below:

Select other formatting options like Background color, Title font, Body font, etc. to customize your blog.

➢ **Pages**

The "Pages" screen allows you to add more pages to your blog, and is displayed on the next page.

Click the **Add a page** link to add another page to your blog.

> ➢ **Advanced**

The "Advanced" screen is displayed below.

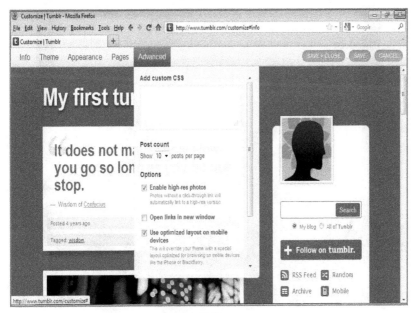

Set the other options for your blog like posts per page, high resolution photos, open links in new window and optimized layout on mobile devices.

At any step during customization, click **Save + Close** to save your settings, close the customization window, and go back to the dashboard. Click **Save** to save the settings and stay on the customization page. Click **Cancel** to cancel customization and go back to the dashboard.

> **Follow People**

You can search your friends and follow them or you can find a topic of your interest and follow the users associated with those topics. The "Follow People" page is displayed below.

➢ **Lookup Contacts**

Find your contacts from Gmail, Yahoo!, Hotmail, AOL, or MSN, and follow them.

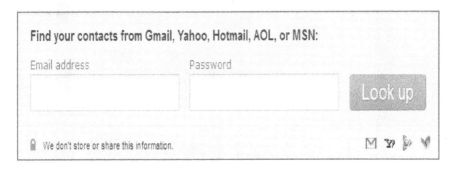

Complete the entries in the fields. The following table provides more information.

This Field	Requires...
Email address	Enter the email address of the email account in which you want to look up. It could be Gmail, Yahoo!, AOL or MSN account.
Password	Enter your email account's password.
Look up	Click **Look up** to find contacts.

Your contacts that are already on Tumblr are displayed. You can follow your friend's blogs.

➢ **Select a Topic and Follow People**

You can select topics, groups you are interested in, find a few people you want to hear from, and follow them. You can get instant updates from industry experts or favorite celebrities by following them.

Select a topic, and the users in that topic are displayed as shown in the figure on the next page.

Move the mouse pointer over the user you want to follow. The **Follow** button appears as shown in the figure below.

Click the **Follow** button to start following the user. You will receive updates from the users you are following in your Tumblr dashboard as shown in the figure below.

Now you are only one step away from completing your Tumblr registration, and that step is email verification as discussed below.

➢ **Email Verification**

Tumblr will perform email authentication to complete your registration. Tumblr will send an email at your email address registered with Tumblr. You will have to log into your email and click on the confirmation link in the email to activate your account.

Log into your webmail and check the email received from Tumblr. The email will appear something like this:

Tumblr verification email

15 Jul 11 12:44:34 🖨 Print

Tumblr <notifications@tumblr.com>   📄 More Mails from this user

Next »

Welcome to Tumblr! We need you to verify your email by clicking on the following link:

http://www.tumblr.com/verify/w7i4kux

Love,
TumblrBot

This message was intended for avcd@in.com.
To change your email settings, use <a href="http://www.tumblr.com/preferences."
target="_blank">http://www.tumblr.com/preferences.</a>
Tumblr's offices are located at 35 East 21st Street, 9th Floor, New York, NY, 10010.

Click or paste the confirmation link in your browser's address bar. The success message will be displayed, which is shown below.

> **Preferences**

Once your account is setup, you can edit your profile from the "Preferences" page. The profile information you provide here will appear in your public profile. It will help those who are following you to identify you. It will also help your friends to search for you on Tumblr.

Click the "Preferences" button in the header as indicated in red in the figure on the next page.

130

The Preferences page is displayed as shown on the next page.

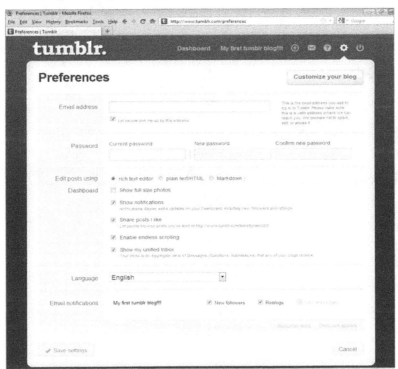

Complete the entries in the fields. The following table provides more information.

This Field	Requires...
Email Address	This is the email address with which you are registered on Tumblr. Select the check box "Let people look me up by this address" to enable people to search you on Tumblr by this email address.
Password	Your current password is displayed. If you want to change your password, enter it as "New password" and "Confirm new password".
Edit Posts Using	Select the method by which you want to edit the posts, "Rich text editor", "plain text/HTML" or "Markdown."
Dashboard	Select the "show full size photos" so that full size photos are displayed in your posts. Select the "show notifications" check box if you want the notifications like new followers and reblogs to be displayed in the dashboard. If you select the "share the posts I like" check box, people will be able to browse the posts you like. Select the "enable endless scrolling" for endless scrolling of your dashboard. Select the "show my unified inbox" to let your inbox show all the suggestions or questions your blogs receive.
Language	Select language from the drop-down box.
Email Notifications	Select the blogs for which you want to receive the notifications. Also select whether you want to receive notifications for New Followers, Reblogs, or New Messages.
Block Other Users	Click here if you want to block any user.
Delete Your Account	Click here if you want to delete your Tumblr account.
Save Settings	Click **Save Settings** button to save your settings.
Cancel	Click **Cancel** to cancel saving the settings.

Congratulations! Your Tumblr account is created, and your Tumblr profile is set up. You are now ready to start using Tumblr.

See the next section of this book entitled "Integrating Social Media" for ideas on how to integrate your Tumblr account with your other social media profiles that are outlined in this book.

Integrating Social Media

One of the strongest benefits of social media is its continually-expanding integration between leading social channels, as well as linking with and complementing your wider Internet networking activity, such as email marketing or online public relations.

There is significant value in linking these four platforms together to boost your online presence and exposure—and also substantial efficiency and time savings for you and your team as you get started with your social media activity.

Each social channel has its own suite of networking tools, software, graphics and shortcuts provided for its users to leverage across other platforms.

How You Can Integrate Your Social Media Activity

Let's summarize just some of the ways that these social media platforms can work and link together to your benefit.

On Facebook:

- Show your Facebook page link via a badge, "Like" button, or widget on your website.
- Include your FB link on your Tumblr blog, in your Twitter bio information (or background artwork), or email newsletter.
- List your Facebook Page URL in your LinkedIn contact information.

On Twitter:

- Use Twitter's own capabilities or a third-party application to automatically post your tweets to your Facebook or LinkedIn profiles.

- Google Search tracks tweets, providing search benefits from your Twitter activity.

- Put a Twitter badge or widget on your website.

On LinkedIn:

- Set up your Twitter feed to automatically upload on your LinkedIn profile, as either a status update or in a sidebar feed.

- Display your blog posts as they are uploaded on Tumblr.

- Show your LinkedIn profile link on your website.

On Tumblr:

- Share your posts via auto-feeds to Facebook and Twitter and set up an RSS (Really Simple Syndication) feed for your blog.

- Use the platform to boost SEO results, with Google optimizing search-friendly Tumblr features, from URLs to sitemaps.

- Email or text posts from your mobile phone.

- Email posts that upload directly to you blog.

- Share anything on the web by using the Tumblr Bookmarklet.

- Google Search tracks some Tumblr elements, providing search benefits from your activity.

Read each User Guide for further technical and marketing set-up guidelines and instructions and make the most of the increasing integration of these huge online communities.

Conclusion

If there is one thing that we've learned about social media in the last several years it's that it isn't going away anytime soon. In fact, the world of social media and online networking is growing larger by the tweet and bigger by the status update. Constantly evolving, social media websites are getting better at reaching out to new users every day.

With millions of people surfing the Internet, it just makes sense that you should establish your professional identity there. Potential employers and clients are only a few clicks away. Build your online profile, make your personal brand recognizable, and begin creating a networking strategy that works for you.

Convenient, fun, and cost effective, sites like Facebook, Twitter, LinkedIn and Tumblr can open up endless networking possibilities to strengthen your professional identity and create the change that you've been looking for.

I wish you the best of luck on your journey and I hope this has been helpful.

Rob Ganjon

Follow me on Twitter: @rganjon

About the Author

Rob is currently a Vice President at American Express in New York and is passionate about the digital revolution currently transforming the way we live and interact with each other – either as consumers, professionals or business owners. In addition to his work at American Express, Rob is an active entrepreneur and involved in various ventures either as a founder, investor or advisor. Currently Rob is the founder of a stealth start-up building a social lifestyle and productivity platform schedule to launch in early 2012.

Rob has a bachelor's degree in finance from Clemson University and an MBA from Columbia Business School. Rob lives in South Orange, New Jersey with his wife, Jessica, and their three children.

Follow Rob on Twitter: @rganjon

Notes

Notes

Notes

Notes